HYMN OF THE UNIVERSE

Pierre Teilhard de Chardin

HYMN
OF
THE
UNIVERSE

Perennial Library
Harper & Row, Publishers
New York, Evanston, San Francisco, London

This book was originally published in 1961 by Editions du Seuil, Paris, and is here reprinted by arrangement.

PREFATORY LETTER
from H. M. Queen Marie-José

Père Teilhard de Chardin, a figure-head in the unfolding of a new cycle in the life of mankind, moves us profoundly not only by the amazing lucidity of his scientific vision but also by his love, his immense love, of God, which enabled him to see, everywhere throughout the created world, what the majority of men are blind to: the constant presence of the Creator. Père Teilhard was far from being a pantheist; but he saw God, the First Cause, present everywhere, and, filled as he was with reverence for the material world, he lived always in direct awareness of the spiritual. The most convincing proof of what some have called the "saintliness of Père Teilhard" is his humility; and his humility is the pledge of the greatness of his love.

January 1961   MARIE-JOSÉ

CONTENTS

TRANSLATOR'S NOTE

In this book it is almost always Père Teilhard the man of prayer rather than the man of science who speaks to us. As Sir Julian Huxley wrote of *The Mass on the World*, it is a "truly poetical essay . . . at one and the same time mystical and realistic, religious and philosophical." This does not mean, of course, that the author ever forgets or betrays his science; what it does mean is that the reader's approach, and response, to these pages must of necessity be quite different from those demanded by the scientific works. The mystic, the poet use language in a way essentially different from that of the scientist.

In his study of St John of the Cross in *The Degrees of Knowledge*, M. Maritain defined this difference with clarity and exactitude in terms of the contrast between the (poetical) language of the mystic and the (scientific) language of the theologian, and pointed out the disastrous results of reading the former as though it were the latter. The aim of scientific language is to provide exactly defined and unambiguous statements *about* reality; that of poetic language is to communicate *reality* itself, as experienced, by means of imagery, evocation, tone, and the ambiguity—or rather ambivalence—of paradox, of symbol. That is not to say that poetic language is nebulous, vague, uncertain: on the contrary, the cutting edge of great poetry is sharper and digs deeper than that of any prose. But we shall never hear what the mystic (or the poet or the musician) has to tell us if we are listening on the wrong wave-length.

"God *needs* man," said Angelus Silesius. If this were a scientific-theological statement it would be an absurdity, just as if Christ's "Lazarus our friend is sleeping" were a scientific-medical statement it would be a falsehood. The theologian has to restate, laboriously and at length, in his own language what is contained in the mystic's flash of intuition. (The words of Silesius come to mind because there are lines in this book which both echo them and elucidate them.) Thus there is no need for us to be alarmed at such ideas as that of God "animating" the world of matter, or of the whole world "becoming incarnate": we shall find plenty of parallels in St Paul and in the traditional theological doctrine of the omnipresence of God. And at the same time it should perhaps be said that, while an acquaintance with Père Teilhard's scientific works must naturally be helpful in understanding fully this present book, it is by no means necessary to know, still less to be in full agreement with, the author's scientific theory in order to be profoundly stirred and illumined by these pages.

The special response from the reader invited by

a book such as this is paralleled by the special demands put upon the translator. Translation must always of course be a rendering not of word for word
but of idea for idea; to be content to transliterate
is merely illiterate. But whereas in translating scientific prose the aim is simply to reproduce with
complete accuracy the author's statements, in
translating "poetic" language the primary aim is not
just to reproduce statements *about* reality but, as
far as may be, to make the same communication *of*
reality—which will mean trying to reproduce something of the author's "tone of voice," something of
the mood and color of the original. And, it may be
added, a poem (unlike a scientific treatise) may
well defy an exact "literal" rendering, even were it
the job of the translator to attempt one. (For instance, quite apart from the untimely echos of
Alice, and of Sir Winston Churchill's first steps with
the Latin primer, which the phrase would arouse,
you just cannot, in English, say "O Matter!") In
this book, then, and especially in the earlier part, I
have sometimes resorted to a slight verbal elaboration, either because there was no alternative if one
was to write English at all, or because two words
seemed necessary to convey the full "poetic" content of one word in the French, or again because a
verbal elaboration seemed more likely to communicate the color (and color is of the essence of vision) of the original. But I think it is true to say
that nowhere have I made any substantial addition
to or alteration of the author's insights and ideas;
and to a great extent, especially in the latter part of
the book, it was in fact possible to cling closely not

only to the sense but also to the wording of the French.

The translation of the Latin in the footnotes follows the Douai version of the Bible.

GERALD VANN, O.P.

INTRODUCTION TO THE MASS ON THE WORLD

This meditation suggested itself to Père Teilhard when, in the course of a scientific expedition, he found himself one day out in the Ordos desert where it was impossible for him to offer Mass. This happened, it seems, on the feast of the Transfiguration,* a feast for which he had a special love. His thoughts therefore turned to the radiation of the eucharistic presence of Christ through the universe. He did not of course confuse that presence, the effect of transubstantiation in the strict sense, with the omnipresence of the divine Word. His faith in the mystery of the Eucharist was not only ardent: it was also as exact as it was firm. But his faith was sufficiently strong and realistic to show him its consequences (or, as he put it, the "prolongations" and

* Père Teilhard could not have written *The Mass on the World* on Easter Sunday 1923, as was reported by friends from Pekin, for he did not reach the desert till August of that year. There was doubtless a confusion between the two feasts of Christ's glory. On a number of occasions Père Teilhard expressed his special love for the feast of the Transfiguration. (Ed. note.)

extensions). At a time when individualism was still, generally speaking, obscuring the fullness of traditional Catholic teaching on this mystery, he wrote: "When Christ comes to one of his faithful it is not simply in order to commune with him as an individual; . . . when, through the mouth of the priest, he says *Hoc est corpus meum,* these words extend beyond the morsel of bread over which they are said: they give birth to the whole mystical body of Christ. The effect of the priestly act extends beyond the consecrated host to the cosmos itself . . . . The entire realm of matter is slowly but irrestibly affected by this great consecration." *

Earlier, in 1917, Père Teilhard had written, in *Le Prêtre*:

"When Christ, extending the process of his incarnation, descends into the bread in order to replace it, his action is not limited to the material morsel which his presence will, for a brief moment, volatilize: this transubstantiation is aureoled with a real though attentuated divinizing of the entire universe. From the particular cosmic element into which he has entered, the activity of the Word goes forth to subdue and to draw into himself all the rest."

Such passages as these not only contain an exact affirmation of the essence of the eucharistic mystery, but also make an equally exact distinction between the essential mystery and the further effects in which its fecundity is manifested: the growth of

* This was written in the same year as *The Mass on the World*.

Christ's mystical body, the consecration of the cosmos. They also bear witness to a plenitude of faith in which Père Teilhard's thought is revealed as being authentically and profoundly in accord with the thought of St Paul. He "shows himself preoccupied above all with giving his daily Mass a *cosmic function* and *planetary dimensions*. . . . This, of course, he considered could be linked up with the most orthodox theology of the holy Eucharist."*

A year after writing *The Mass on the World*, Père Teilhard further defined his thought, in *Mon Univers*: "To interpret adequately the fundamental position of the Eucharist in the economy of the world . . . it is, I think, necessary that Christian thought and Christian prayer should give great importance to the real and physical extensions of the eucharistic Presence. . . . As we properly use the term "our bodies" to signify the localized center of our spiritual radiations . . . so it must be said that in its initial and primary meaning the term "Body of Christ" is limited, in this context, to the consecrated species of Bread and Wine. But . . . the host is comparable to a blazing fire whose flames spread out like rays all round it."

N. M. WILDIERS, S.T.D.

* Nicolas Corte: *The Life and Soul of Teilhard de Chardin* (Eng. trans. Barrie & Rockliff, 1960), p. 26.

THE MASS
ON THE WORLD

The Offering

Since once again, Lord—though this time not in the forests of the Aisne but in the steppes of Asia—I have neither bread, nor wine, nor altar, I will raise myself beyond these symbols, up to the pure majesty of the real itself; I, your priest, will make the whole earth my altar and on it will offer you all the labors and sufferings of the world.

Over there, on the horizon, the sun has just touched with light the outermost fringe of the eastern sky. Once again, beneath this moving sheet of fire, the living surface of the earth wakes and trembles, and once again begins its fearful travail. I will place on my paten, O God, the harvest to be won by this renewal of labor. Into my chalice I shall pour all the sap which is to be pressed out this day from the earth's fruits.

My paten and my chalice are the depths of a soul laid widely open to all the forces which in a moment will rise up from every corner of the earth and converge upon the Spirit. Grant me the remembrance and the mystic presence of all those whom the light is now awakening to the new day.

My paten and my chalice are the depths of a soul laid widely open to all the forces which in a moment will rise up from every corner of the earth and converge upon the Spirit. Grant me the remembrance and the mystic presence of all those whom the light is now awakening to the new day.

One by one, Lord, I see and I love all those whom you have given me to sustain and charm my life. One by one also I number all those who make up that other beloved family which has gradually surrounded me, its unity fashioned out of the most disparate elements, with affinities of the heart, of scientific research and of thought. And again one by one—more vaguely it is true, yet all inclusively —I call before me the whole vast anonymous army of living humanity; those who surround me and support me though I do not know them; those who come, and those who go; above all, those who in office, laboratory and factory, through their vision of truth or despite their error, truly believe in the progress of earthly reality and who today will take up again their impassioned pursuit of the light.

This restless multitude, confused or orderly, the immensity of which terrifies us; this ocean of humanity whose slow, monotonous wave-flows trouble the hearts even of those whose faith is most firm: it is to this deep that I thus desire all the fibers of my being should respond. All the things in the world to which this day will bring increase; all those that will diminish; all those too that will die: all of them, Lord, I try to gather into my arms, so as to hold them out to you in offering. This is the material of my sacrifice; the only material you desire.

Once upon a time men took into your temple the first fruits of their harvests, the flower of their flocks. But the offering you really want, the offer-

ing you mysteriously need every day to appease
your hunger, to slake your thirst is nothing less
than the growth of the world borne ever onwards
in the stream of universal becoming.

Receive, O Lord, this all-embracing host which
your whole creation, moved by your magnetism,
offers you at this dawn of a new day.

This bread, our toil, is of itself, I know, but an
immense fragmentation; this wine, our pain, is no
more, I know, than a draught that dissolves. Yet in
the very depths of this formless mass you have implanted—and this I am sure of, for I sense it—a desire, irresistible, hallowing, which makes us cry out,
believer and unbeliever alike: "Lord, make us *one*."

Because, my God, though I lack the soul-zeal and
the sublime integrity of your saints, I yet have re-
ceived from you an overwhelming sympathy for all
that stirs within the dark mass of matter; because I
know myself to be irremediably less a child of
heaven than a son of earth; therefore I will this
morning climb up in spirit to the high places, bearing with me the hopes and the miseries of my
mother; and there—empowered by that priesthood
which you alone (as I firmly believe) have bestowed on me—upon all that in the world of
human flesh is now about to be born or to die beneath the rising sun I will call down the Fire.

Fire over the Earth

Fire, the source of being: we cling so tenaciously to
the illusion that fire comes forth from the depths of
the earth and that its flames grow progressively

brighter as it pours along the radiant furrows of life's tillage. Lord, in your mercy you gave me to see that this idea is false, and that I must overthrow it if I were ever to have sight of you.

In the beginning was *Power*, intelligent, loving, energizing. In the beginning was the *Word*, supremely capable of mastering and molding whatever might come into being in the world of matter. In the beginning there were not coldness and darkness: there was the *Fire*. This is the truth.

So, far from light emerging gradually out of the womb of our darkness, it is the Light, existing before all else was made which, patiently, surely, eliminates our darkness. As for us creatures, of ourselves we are but emptiness and obscurity. But you, my God, are the inmost depths, the stability of that eternal *milieu*, without duration or space, in which our cosmos emerges gradually into being and grows gradually to its final completeness, as it loses those boundaries which to our eyes seem so immense. Everything is being; everywhere there is being and nothing but being, save in the fragmentation of creatures and the clash of their atoms.

Blazing Spirit, Fire, personal, super-substantial, the consummation of a union so immeasurably more lovely and more desirable than that destructive fusion of which all the pantheists dream: be pleased yet once again to come down and breathe a soul into the newly formed, fragile film of matter with which this day the world is to be freshly clothed.

I know we cannot forestall, still less dictate to

you, even the smallest of your actions; from you alone comes all initiative—and this applies in the first place to my prayer.

Radiant Word, blazing Power, you who mold the manifold so as to breathe your life into it; I pray you, lay on us those your hands—powerful, considerate, omnipresent, those hands which do not (like our human hands) touch now here, now there, but which plunge into the depths and the totality, present and past, of things so as to reach us simultaneously through all that is most immense and most inward within us and around us.

May the might of those invincible hands direct and transfigure for the great world you have in mind that earthly travail which I have gathered into my heart and now offer you in its entirety. Remold it, rectify it, recast it down to the depths from whence it springs. You know how your creatures can come into being only, like shoot from stem, as part of an endlessly renewed process of evolution.

Do you now therefore, speaking through my lips, pronounce over this earthly travail your twofold efficacious word: the word without which all that our wisdom and our experience have built up must totter and crumble—the word through which all our most far-reaching speculations and our encounter with the universe are come together into a unity. Over every living thing which is to spring up, to grow, to flower, to ripen during this day say again the words: This is my Body. And over every death-force which waits in readiness to corrode, to wither, to cut down, speak again your commanding words which express the supreme mystery of faith: This is my Blood.*

Fire in the Earth

It is done.

Once again the Fire has penetrated the earth.

Not with sudden crash of thunderbolt, riving the mountain-tops: does the Master break down doors to enter his own home? Without earthquake, or thunderclap: the flame has lit up the whole world from within. All things individually and collectively are penetrated and flooded by it, from the inmost core of the tiniest atom to the mighty sweep of the most universal laws of being: so naturally has it flooded every element, every energy, every connecting link in the unity of our cosmos; that one

---

* As was pointed out in the *Introduction*, there is no confusion here between transubstantiation in the strict sense and the universal presence of the Word: as the author states explicitly in *Le Prêtre*, "The central mystery of transubstantiation is aureoled by a divinization, real though attenuated, of all the universe." From the cosmic element into which he has entered through his incarnation and in which he dwells eucharistically, "the Word acts upon everything else to subdue and assimilate it to himself." (Ed. note.)

might suppose the cosmos to have burst spontaneously into flame.

In the new humanity which is begotten today the Word prolongs the unending act of his own birth; and by virtue of his immersion in the world's womb the great waters of the kingdom of matter have, without even a ripple, been endued with life. No visible tremor marks this inexpressible transformation; and yet, mysteriously and in very truth, at the touch of the supersubstantial Word the immense host which is the universe is made flesh. Through your own incarnation, my God, all matter is henceforth incarnate.

Through our thoughts and our human experiences, we long ago became aware of the strange properties which make the universe so like our flesh:

like the flesh it attracts us by the charm which lies in the mystery of its curves and folds and in the depths of its eyes;

like the flesh it disintegrates and eludes us when submitted to our analyses or to our fallings off and in the process of its own perdurance;

as with the flesh, it can only be embraced in the endless reaching out to attain what lies beyond the confines of what has been given to us.

All of us, Lord, from the moment we are born feel within us this disturbing mixture of remoteness and nearness; and in our heritage of sorrow and hope, passed down to us through the ages, there is no yearning more desolate than that which makes us weep with vexation and desire as we stand in the midst of the Presence which hovers about us nameless and impalpable and is dwelling in all things. *Si forte attrectent eum.**

Now, Lord, through the consecration of the

---

* "That they [all mankind] should seek God, if happily they may feel after him or find him. . . ." (Acts 17.27.)

world the luminosity and fragrance which suffuse
the universe take on for me the lineaments of a
body and a face—in you. What my mind glimpsed
through its hesitant explorations, what my heart
craved with so little expectation of fulfillment, you
now magnificently unfold for me: the fact that your
creatures are not merely so linked together in soli-
darity that none can exist unless all the rest surround it, but that all are so dependent on a single
central reality that a true life, borne in common by
them all, gives them ultimately their consistence
and their unity.

Shatter, my God, through the daring of your revelation the childishly timid outlook that can con-
ceive of nothing greater or more vital in the world
than the pitiable perfection of our human organism. On the road to a bolder comprehension of the
universe the children of this world day by day out-
distance the masters of Israel; but do you, Lord
Jesus, "in whom all things subsist," show yourself to
those who love you as the higher Soul and the
physical center of your creation. Are you not well
aware that for us this is a question of life or death?
As for me, if I could not believe that your real Presence animates and makes tractable and enkindles
even the very least of the energies which invade me
or brush past me, would I not die of cold?

I thank you, my God, for having in a thousand
different ways led my eyes to discover the immense
simplicity of things. Little by little, through the irresistible development of those yearnings you implanted in me as a child, through the influence of

gifted friends who entered my life at certain moments to bring light and strength to my mind, and through the awakenings of spirit I owe to the successive initiations, gentle and terrible, which you caused me to undergo: through all these I have been brought to the point where I can no longer see anything, nor any longer breathe, outside that *milieu* in which all is made one.

At this moment when your life has just poured with superabundant vigor into the sacrament of the world, I shall savor with heightened consciousness the intense yet tranquil rapture of a vision whose coherence and harmonies I can never exhaust.

What I experience as I stand in face of—and in the very depths of—this world which your flesh has assimilated, this world which has become your flesh, my God, is not the absorption of the monist who yearns to be dissolved into the unity of things, nor the emotion felt by the pagan as he lies prostrate before a tangible divinity, nor yet the passive self-abandonment of the quietist tossed hither and thither at the mercy of mystical impulses. From each of these modes of thought I take something of their motive force while avoiding their pitfalls: the approach determined for me by your omnipresence is a wonderful synthesis wherein three of the most formidable passions that can unlock the human heart rectify each other as they mingle: like the monist I plunge into the all-inclusive One; but the One is so perfect that as it receives me and I lose myself in it I can find in it the ultimate perfection of my own individuality;

like the pagan I worship a God who can be touched; and I do indeed touch him—this God—over the whole surface and in the depths of that world of matter which confines me: but to take hold of him as I would wish (simply in order not to stop touching him), I must go always on and on through and beyond each undertaking, unable to rest in anything, borne onwards at each moment by creatures and at each moment going beyond them, in a continuing welcoming of them and a continuing detachment from them;

like the quietist I allow myself with delight to be cradled in the divine fantasy: but at the same time I know that the divine will, will only be revealed to me at each moment if I exert myself to the utmost: I shall only touch God in the world of matter, when, like Jacob, I have been vanquished by him.

Thus, because the ultimate objective, the totality to which my nature is attuned has been made manifest to me, the powers of my being begin spontaneously to vibrate in accord with a single note of incredible richness wherein I can distinguish the most discordant tendencies effortlessly resolved: the excitement of action and the delight of passivity: the joy of possessing and the thrill of reaching out beyond what one possesses; the pride in growing and the happiness of being lost in what is greater than oneself.

Rich with the sap of the world, I rise up towards the Spirit whose vesture is the magnificence of the material universe but who smiles at me from far beyond all victories; and, lost in the mystery of the flesh of God, I cannot tell which is the more radiant bliss: to have found the Word and so be able to achieve the mastery of matter, or to have mastered matter and so be able to attain and submit to the light of God.

Grant, Lord, that your descent into the universal Species may not be for me just something loved and cherished, like the fruit of some philosophical speculation, but may become for me truly a real Presence. Whether we like it or not by power and by right you are incarnate in the world, and we are all of us dependent upon you. But in fact you are far, and how far, from being equally close to us all. We are all of us together carried in the one world-womb; yet each of us is our own little microcosm in which the Incarnation is wrought independently with degrees of intensity, and shades that are incommunicable. And that is why, in our prayer at the altar, we ask that the consecration may be brought about *for us*: *Ut nobis Corpus et Sanguis fiat . . .*° If I firmly believe that everything around me is the body and blood of the Word,°° then for me (and in one sense for me alone) is brought about that marvelous "diaphany" which causes the luminous warmth of a single life to be objectively discernible in and to shine forth from

° "That it may become for us the Body and Blood of your dearly loved Son, our Lord Jesus Christ."

°° Through the "physical and overmastering" contact of him whose appanage it is to be able *omnia sibi subicere* ["to subdue all things unto himself." Phil. 3.21]. (*Le Milieu Divin*, Eng. trans. p. 114.)

the depths of every event, every element: whereas if, unhappily, my faith should flag, at once the light is quenched and everything becomes darkened, everything disintegrates.

You have come down, Lord, into this day which is now beginning. But alas, how infinitely different in degree is your presence for one and another of us in the events which are now preparing and which all of us together will experience! In the very same circumstances which are soon to surround me and my fellowmen you may be present in small measure, in great measure, more and more or not at all.

Therefore, Lord, that no poison may harm me this day, no death destroy me, no wine befuddle me, that in every creature I may discover and sense you, I beg you: give me faith.

Communion

If the Fire has come down into the heart of the world it is, in the last resort, to lay hold on me and to absorb me. Henceforth I cannot be content simply to contemplate it or, by my steadfast faith, to intensify its ardency more and more in the world around me. What I must do, when I have taken part with all my energies in the consecration which causes its flames to leap forth, is to consent to the communion which will enable it to find in me the food it has come in the last resort to seek.

So, my God, I prostrate myself before your presence in the universe which has now become living flame: beneath the lineaments of all that I shall encounter this day, all that happens to me, all that I achieve, it is you I desire, you I await.

It is a terrifying thing to have been born: I mean, to find oneself, without having willed it, swept irrevocably along on a torrent of fearful energy which seems as though it wished to destroy everything it carries with it.

What I want, my God, is that by a reversal of forces which you alone can bring about, my terror in face of the nameless changes destined to renew my being may be turned into an overflowing joy at being transformed into you.

First of all I shall stretch out my hand unhesitatingly towards the fiery bread which you set before me. This bread, in which you have planted the seed of all that is to develop in the future, I recognize as containing the source and the secret of that destiny you have chosen for me. To take it is, I know, to surrender myself to forces which will tear me away painfully from myself in order to drive me into danger, into laborious undertakings, into a constant renewal of ideas, into an austere detachment where my affections are concerned. To eat it is to acquire a taste and an affinity for that which in everything is above everything—a taste and an affinity which will henceforward make impossible for me all the joys by which my life has been warmed. Lord Jesus, I am willing to be possessed by you, to be bound to your body and led by its inexpressible power towards those solitary heights which by myself I should never dare to climb. Instinctively, like all mankind, I would rather set up my tent here below on some hilltop of my own choosing. I am afraid, too, like all my fellowmen, of the future too heavy with mystery and too wholly new, towards which time is driving me. Then like these men I wonder anxiously where life is leading me. . . . May this communion of bread with the Christ clothed in the powers which dilate the world free me from my timidities and my heedlessness! In the whirlpool of conflicts and energies out of which must develop my power to apprehend and experience your holy presence, I throw myself, my God, on your word. The man who is filled with an impassioned love of Jesus hidden in the forces which bring increase to the earth, him the earth will lift up, like a mother, in the immensity of her arms, and will enable him to contemplate the face of God.

If your kingdom, my God, were of this world, I could possess you simply by surrendering myself to the forces which cause us, through suffering and dying, to grow visibly in stature—us or that which is dearer to us than ourselves. But because the term towards which the earth is moving lies not merely beyond each individual thing but beyond the totality of things; because the world travails, not to bring forth from within itself some supreme reality, but to find its consummation through a union with a preexistent Being; it follows that man can never reach the blazing center of the universe simply by living more and more for himself nor even by spending his life in the service of some earthly cause however great. The world can never be definitively united with you, Lord, save by a sort of reversal, a turning about, an *excentration*, which must involve the temporary collapse not merely of all individual achievements but even of everything that looks like an advancement for humanity. If my being is ever to be decisively attached to yours, there must first die in me not merely the monad ego but also the world: in other words I must first pass through an agonizing phase of diminution for which no tangible compensation will be given me. That is why, pouring into my chalice the bitterness of all separations, of all limitations, and of all sterile fallings away, you then hold it out to me. "Drink ye all of this."

How could I refuse this chalice, Lord, now that through the bread you have given me there has crept into the marrow of my being an inextinguishable longing to be united with you beyond life; through death? The consecration of the world would have remained incomplete, a moment ago, had you not with special love vitalized for those who believe, not only the life-bringing forces, but also those which bring death. My communion would be incomplete—would, quite simply, not be Christian—if, together with the gains which this new day brings me, I did not also accept, in my own name and in the name of the world as the most immediate sharing in your own being, those processes, hidden or manifest, of enfeeblement, of aging, of death, which unceasingly consume the universe, to its salvation or its condemnation. My God, I deliver myself up with utter abandon to those fearful forces of dissolution which, I blindly believe, will this day cause my narrow ego to be replaced by your divine presence. The man who is filled with an impassioned love for Jesus hidden in the forces which bring death to the earth, him the earth will clasp in the immensity of her arms as her strength fails, and with her he will awaken in the bosom of God.

Prayer

Lord Jesus, now that beneath those world forces you have become truly and physically everything for me, everything about me, everything within me, I shall gather into a single prayer both my delight in what I have and my thirst for what I lack; and following the lead of your great servant I shall repeat those enflamed words in which, I firmly believe, the Christianity of tomorrow will find its increasingly clear portrayal:

"Lord, lock me up in the deepest depths of your heart; and then, holding me there, burn me, purify me, set me on fire, sublimate me, till I become utterly what you would have me be, through the utter annihilation of my ego." *

Tu autem, Domine mi, include me in imis visceri-

---

* The term "ego" is used here (in contrast to the "true self") to denote the proud, defiant self-reliance, the attempted autonomy, of man in revolt against God. Only through the death of the ego can the true self be liberated; for man is truly himself only when he has replaced his ego-centricity by theocentricity and thus found his true self by looking for it in God, in whom alone we "live and move and have our being." (Tr. note.)

bus Cordis tui. Atque ibi me detine, excoque, ex-
purga, accende, ignifac, sublima, ad purissimum
Cordis tui gustum atque placitum, ad puram an-
nihilationem meam.*

"Lord." Yes, at last, through the twofold mystery
of this universal consecration and communion I
have found one to whom I can wholeheartedly give
this name. As long as I could see—or dared see—in
you, Lord Jesus, only the man who lived two thousand years ago, the sublime moral teacher, the
Friend, the Brother, my love remained timid and
constrained. Friends, brothers, wise men: have we
not many of these around us, great souls, chosen
souls, and much closer to us? And then can man
ever give himself utterly to a nature which is
purely human? Always from the very first it was
the world, greater than all the elements which
make up the world, that I was in love with; and
never before was there anyone before whom I
could in honesty bow down. And so for a long time,
even though I believed, I strayed, not knowing
what it was I loved. But now, Master, today, when
through the manifestation of those superhuman
powers with which your resurrection endowed you
you shine forth from within all the forces of the
earth and so become visible to me, now I recognize
you as my Sovereign, and with delight I surrender
myself to you.

How strange, my God, are the processes your

* "And thou, my Lord, enfold me in the depths of thy Heart.
And there keep me, refine, purge, kindle, set on fire, raise
aloft, according to the most pure desire of thy Heart, and
for my cleansing extinction."

Spirit initiates! When, two centuries ago, your Church began to feel the particular power of your heart, it might have seemed that what was captivating men's souls was the fact of their finding in you an element even more determinate, more circumscribed, than your humanity as a whole. But now on the contrary a swift reversal is making us aware that your main purpose in this revealing to us of your heart was to enable our love to escape from the constrictions of the too narrow, too precise, too limited image of you which we had fashioned for ourselves. What I discern in your breast is simply a furnace of fire; and the more I fix my gaze on its ardency the more it seems to me that all around it the contours of your body melt away and become enlarged beyond all measure, till the only features I can distinguish in you are those of the face of a world which has burst into flame.

Glorious Lord Christ: the divine influence secretly diffused and active in the depths of matter, and the dazzling center where all the innumerable fibers of the manifold meet; power as implacable as the world and as warm as life; you whose forehead is of the whiteness of snow, whose eyes are of fire, and whose feet are brighter than molten gold; you whose hands imprison the stars; you who are the first and the last, the living and the dead and the risen again; you who gather into your exuberant unity every beauty, every affinity, every energy, every mode of existence; it is you to whom my being cried out with a desire as vast as the universe, "In truth you are my Lord and my God."

"Lord, lock me up within you": yes indeed I believe—and this belief is so strong that it has become one of the supports of my inner life—that an "exterior darkness" which was wholly outside you would be pure nothingness. Nothing, Lord Jesus, can subsist outside of your flesh; so that even those who have been cast out from your love are still, unhappily for them, the beneficiaries of your presence upholding them in existence. All of us, inescapably, exist in you, the universal *milieu* in which and through which all things live and have their being. But precisely because we are not self-contained ready-made entities which can be conceived equally well as being near to you or remote from you; precisely because in us the self-subsistent individual who is united to you grows only insofar as the union itself grows, that union whereby we are given more and more completely to you: I beg you, Lord, in the name of all that is most vital in my being, to hearken to the desire of this thing that I dare to call *my* soul even though I realize more and more every day how much greater it is than myself, and, to slake my thirst for life, draw me—through the successive zones of your deepest substance—into the secret recesses of your inmost heart.

The deeper the level at which one encounters you, Master, the more one realizes the universality of your influence. This is the criterion by which I can judge at each moment how far I have progressed within you. When all the things around me, while preserving their own individual contours, their own special savors, nevertheless appear to me as animated by a single secret spirit and therefore as diffused and intermingled within a single element, infinitely close, infinitely remote; and when, locked within the jealous intimacy of a divine sanctuary, I yet feel myself to be wandering at large in the empyrean of all created beings: then I shall know that I am approaching that central point where the heart of the world is caught in the descending radiance of the heart of God.

And then, Lord, at that point where all things are set ablaze, do you act upon me through the united flames of all those internal and external influences which, were I less close to you, would be neutral or ambivalent or hostile, but which when animated by an Energy *quae possit sibi omnia subjicere** become, in the physical depths of your heart, the angels of your triumphant activity. Through a marvelous combination of your divine magnetism with the charm and the inadequacy of creatures, with their sweetness and their malice, the disappointing weakness and their terrifying power, do you fill my heart alternately with exaltation and with distaste; teach it the true meaning of purity: not a debilitating separation from all created reality but an impulse carrying one through all forms of created beauty; show it the true nature of charity: not a sterile fear of doing wrong but a vigorous determination that all of us together shall break open the doors of life; and give it finally—give it above all—through an ever-increasing awareness of your omnipresence, a blessed desire to go on advancing, discovering, fashioning and experi-

* "Which is able to subdue all things unto itself."

encing the world so as to penetrate even further and further into yourself.

For me, my God, all joy and all achievement, the very purpose of my being and all my love of life, all depend on this one basic vision of the union between yourself and the universe. Let others, fulfilling a function more august than mine, proclaim your splendors as pure Spirit; as for me, dominated as I am by a vocation which springs from the inmost fibers of my being, I have no desire, I have no ability, to proclaim anything except the innumerable prolongations of your incarnate Being in the world of matter; I can preach only the mystery of your flesh, you the Soul shining forth through all that surrounds us.

It is to your body in this its fullest extension— that is, to the world become through your power and my faith the glorious living crucible in which everything melts away in order to be born anew; it is to this that I dedicate myself with all the resources which your creative magnetism has brought forth in me: with the all too feeble resources of my scientific knowledge, with my religious vows, with my priesthood, and (most dear to me) with my deepest human convictions. It is in this dedication, Lord Jesus, I desire to live, in this I desire to die.

Ordos 1923

CHRIST
IN THE WORLD
OF MATTER

THREE STORIES IN
THE STYLE OF BENSON*

My friend** is dead, he who drank of life everywhere as at a sacred spring. His heart burned
within him. His body lies hidden in the earth in
front of Verdun. Now therefore I can repeat some
of those words with which he initiated me one
evening into that intense vision which gave light
and peace to his life.

"You want to know," he said, "how the universe,
in all its power and multiplicity, came to assume
for me the lineaments of the face of Christ? This
came about gradually; and it is difficult to find
words in which to analyze life-renewing intuitions
such as these; still, I can tell you about some of the
experiences through which the light of this aware-

---

* Père Teilhard sometimes called these stories *histoires*,
sometimes *contes*, written in the manner of Benson: a story
about mysticism by R. H. Benson had made a lasting impression on him. (Cf. *Le Milieu Divin*, Eng. trans. p. 124.)
(Ed. note.)

** In these stories, too intimate in character for the author
not to feel the need to disguise his identity, the "friend" is
clearly himself. (Ed. note.)

ness gradually entered into my soul as though at the gradual, jerky raising of a curtain. . . ."

The Picture

"At that time," he began, "my mind was preoccupied with a problem partly philosophical, partly aesthetic. I was thinking: Suppose Christ should deign to appear here before me, what would he look like? How would he be dressed? Above all, in what manner would he take his place visibly in the realm of matter, and how would he stand out against the objects surrounding him? . . . And confusedly I found myself saddened and shocked at the idea that the body of Christ could stand in the midst of a crowd of inferior bodies on the world's stage without their sensing and recognizing, through some perceptible change, this Intensity so close beside them.

"Meanwhile my gaze had come to rest without conscious intention on a picture representing Christ offering his heart to men. The picture was hanging in front of me on the wall of a church into which I had gone to pray. So, pursuing my train of thought, I began to ask myself how an artist could contrive to represent the holy humanity of Jesus without imposing on his body a fixity, a too precise definition, which would seem to isolate him from all other men, and without giving to his face a too individual expression so that, while being beautiful, its beauty would be of a particular kind, excluding all other kinds.

"It was, then, as I was keenly pondering over

these things and looking at the picture, that my vision began. To tell the truth, I cannot say at what precise moment it began, for it had already reached a certain degree of intensity when I became conscious of it. The fact remains that as I allowed my gaze to wander over the figure's outlines I suddenly became aware that these were *melting away:* they were dissolving, but in a special manner, hard to describe in words. When I tried to hold in my gaze the outline of the figure of Christ it seemed to me to be clearly defined; but then, if I let this effort relax, at once these contours, and the folds of Christ's garment, the luster of his hair and the bloom of his flesh, all seemed to merge as it were (though without vanishing away) into the rest of the picture. It was as though the planes which marked off the figure of Christ from the world surrounding it were melting into a single vibrant surface whereon all demarcations vanished.

"It seems to me that this transformation began at one particular point on the outer edge of the figure; and that it flowed on thence until it had affected its entire outline. This at least is how the process appeared to me to be taking place. From this initial moment, moreover, the metamorphosis spread rapidly until it had affected everything.

"First of all I perceived that the vibrant atmosphere which surrounded Christ like an aureole was no longer confined to a narrow space about him, but radiated outwards to infinity. Through this there passed from time to time what seemed like trails of phosphorescence, indicating a continuous gushing forth to the outermost spheres of the realm of matter and delineating a sort of blood stream or nervous system running through the totality of life.

"*The entire universe was vibrant!* And yet, when I directed my gaze to particular objects, one by one, I found them still as clearly defined as ever in their undiminished individuality.

"All this movement seemed to emanate from Christ, and above all from his heart. And it was while I was attempting to trace the emanation to its source and to capture its rhythm that, as my attention returned to the portrait itself, I saw the vision mount rapidly to its climax.

"I notice I have forgotten to tell you about Christ's garments. They had that luminosity we read of in the account of the Transfiguration; but what struck me most of all was the fact that no weaver's hand had fashioned them—unless the hands of angels are those of Nature. No coarsely spun threads composed their weft; rather it was matter, a bloom of matter, which had spontaneously woven a marvelous stuff out of the inmost depths of its substance; and it seemed as though I could see the stitches running on and on indefinitely, and harmoniously blending together in to a natural design which profoundly affected them in their own nature.

"But, as you will understand, I could spare only a passing glance for this garment so marvelously woven by the continuous cooperation of all the energies and the whole order of matter: it was the transfigured face of the Master that drew and held captive my entire attention.

"You have often at nighttime seen how certain stars change their color from the gleam of blood-red pearls to the luster of violet velvet. You have seen, too, the play of colors on a transparent bubble. So it was that on the unchanging face of Jesus there shone, in an indescribable shimmer or iridescence, all the radiant hues of all our modes of beauty. I cannot say whether this took place in answer to my desires or in obedience to the good pleasure of him who knew and directed my desires; what is certain is that these innumerable gradations of majesty, of sweetness, or irresistible appeal, following one another or becoming transformed and melting into one another, together made up a harmony which brought me complete satiety.

"And always, beneath this moving surface, upholding it and at the same time gathering it into a higher unity, there hovered the incommunicable beauty of Christ himself. Yet that beauty was something I divined rather than perceived; for whenever I tried to pierce through the covering of inferior beauties which hid it from me, at once other individual and fragmentary beauties rose up before me and formed another veil over the true Beauty even while kindling my desire for it and giving me a foretaste of it.

"It was the whole face that shone in this way. But the center of the radiance and the iridescence was hidden in the transfigured portrait's eyes.

"Over the glorious depths of those eyes there passed in rainbow hues the reflection—unless indeed it were the creative prototype, the Idea—of everything that has power to charm us, everything

that has life. . . . And the luminous simplicity of the
fire which flashed from them changed, as I struggled to master it, into an inexhaustible complexity
wherein were gathered all the glances that have
ever warmed and mirrored back a human heart.
Thus, for example, these eyes which at first were so
gentle and filled with pity that I thought my
mother stood before me, became an instant later,
like those of a woman, passionate and filled with
the power to subdue, yet at the same time so im-
periously pure that under their domination it
would have been physically impossible for the
emotions to go astray. And then they changed
again, and became filled with a noble, virile
majesty, similar to that which one sees in the eyes
of men of great courage or refinement or strength,
but incomparably more lofty to behold and more
delightful to submit to.

"This scintillation of diverse beauties was so
complete, so captivating, and also so swift that I
felt it touch and penetrate all my powers simultaneously, so that the very core of my being vibrated
in response to it, sounding a unique note of expansion and happiness.

"Now while I was ardently gazing deep into the
pupils of Christ's eyes, which had become abysses
of fiery, fascinating life, suddenly I beheld rising
up from the depths of those same eyes what
seemed like a cloud, blurring and blending all that
variety I have been describing to you. Little by little an extraordinary expression, of great intensity,
spread over the diverse shades of meaning which

the divine eyes revealed, first of all permeating them and then finally absorbing them all. . . .

"And I stood dumbfounded.

"For this final expression, which had dominated and gathered up into itself all the others, was *indecipherable*. I simply could not tell whether it denoted an indescribable agony or a superabundance of triumphant joy. I only know that since that moment I thought I caught a glimpse of it once again—in the glance of a dying soldier.

"In an instant my eyes were bedimmed with tears. And then, when I was once again able to look at it, the painting of Christ on the church wall had assumed once again its too precise definition and its fixity of feature."

The Monstrance

When he had reached the end of his narrative my friend remained for some time silent and lost in thought, his clasped hands resting in a characteristic attitude on his crossed knees. The light was fading. I pressed a switch, and the lamp on my desk lit up. It was a very pretty lamp; its pedestal and shade were made of diaphanous sea-green glass, and the bulbs were so ingeniously placed that the entire mass of crystal and the designs which decorated it were illumined from within.

My friend gave a start; and I noticed that his gaze remained fixed on the lamp, as though to draw from it his memories of the past, as he began again to confide in me.

"On another occasion," he said, "I was again in a church and had just knelt down before the Blessed Sacrament exposed in a monstrance when I experienced a very strange impression.

"You must, I feel sure, have observed that optical illusion which makes a bright spot against a dark background seem to expand and grow bigger? It was something of this sort that I experienced as I gazed at the host, its white shape standing out sharply, despite the candles on the altar, against the darkness of the choir. At least, that is what happened to begin with; later on, as you shall hear, my experience assumed proportions which no physical analogy could express.

"I had then the impression as I gazed at the host that its surface was gradually spreading out like a spot of oil but of course much more swiftly and luminously. At the beginning it seemed to me that I alone had noticed any change, and that it was taking place without awakening any desire or encountering any obstacle. But little by little, as the white orb grew and grew in space till it seemed to be drawing quite close to me, I heard a subdued sound, an immeasurable murmur, as when the rising tide extends its silver waves over the world of the algae which tremble and dilate at its approach, or when the burning heather crackles as fire spreads over the heath.

"Thus in the midst of a great sigh suggestive both of an awakening and of a plaint the flow of whiteness enveloped me, passed beyond me, overran everything. At the same time everything, though drowned in this whiteness, preserved its own proper shape, its own autonomous movement; for the whiteness did not efface the features or change the nature of anything, but penetrated objects at the core of their being, at a level more profound even than their own life. It was as though a milky brightness were illuminating the universe from within, and everything were fashioned of the same kind of translucent flesh.

"You see, when you switched on the lamp just now and the glass which had been dark became bright and fluorescent, I recalled how the world had appeared to me then; and indeed it was this association of images which prompted me to tell you this story.

"So, through the mysterious expansion of the host the whole world had become incandescent, had itself become like a single giant host. One would have said that, under the influence of this inner light which penetrated it, its fibers were stretched to breaking point and all the energies within them were strained to the utmost. And I was thinking that already in this opening out of its activity the cosmos had attained its plenitude when I became aware that a much more fundamental process was going on within it.

"From moment to moment sparkling drops of pure metal were forming on the inner surface of things and then falling into the heart of this profound light, in which they vanished; and at the same time a certain amount of dross was being volatilized: a transformation was taking place in the domain of love, dilating, purifying and gathering together every power-to-love which the universe contains.

"This I could realize the more easily inasmuch as its influence was operative in me myself as well as in other things: *the white glow was active;* the whiteness was consuming all things from within themselves. It had penetrated, through the channels of matter, into the inmost depths of all hearts and then had dilated them to breaking point, only in order to take back into itself the substance of their affections and passions. And now that it had established its hold on them it was irresistibly pulling back towards its center all the waves that had spread outwards from it, laden now with the purest honey of all loves.

"And in actual fact the immense host, having given life to everything and purified everything, *was now slowly contracting;* and the treasures it was drawing into itself were joyously pressed close together within its living light.

"When a wave recedes or a flame dies down, the area which has been covered for a moment by sea or fire is marked by the shining pools, the glowing embers, which remain. In the same way, as the host closed in on itself like a flower closing its petals, certain refractory elements in the universe remained behind, outside it, in the exterior darkness. There was indeed still something which lit them, but it was a heart of perverted light, corrosive, poisonous; these rebellious elements burned like torches or glowed red like embers.

"I heard then the *Ave verum* being sung.

"The white host was enclosed once again in the golden monstrance; around it candles were burning, stabbing the darkness, and here and there the sanctuary lamps threw out their crimson glow."

The Pyx

As I listened to my friend my heart began to burn within me and my mind awoke to a new and higher vision of things. I began to realize vaguely that the multiplicity of evolutions into which the world process seems to us to be split up is in fact fundamentally the working out of one single great mystery; and this first glimpse of light caused me, I know not why, to tremble in the depths of my soul. But I was so accustomed to separating reality into different planes and categories of thought that I soon found myself lost in this spectacle, still new and strange to my tyro mind, of a cosmos in which the dimensions of divine reality, of spirit, and of matter were also intimately mingled.

Seeing that I was waiting anxiously for further enlightenment, my friend went on:

"The last story I would like to tell you concerns an experience which happened to me just recently. This time, as you'll see, it was not a question of vision properly so called: it was a more general impression which affected, and still affects, my whole being.

"This is what happened.

"At that time my regiment was in line on the Avocourt plateau. The German attack on Verdun was still going on, and fighting was heavy on this side of the Meuse. So, like many priests during battle, I was carrying on me the eucharistic Species in a little pyx shaped like a watch.

"One morning, when there was an almost complete lull in the trenches, I went down into my dugout and there, as I withdrew into a sort of meditation, my thoughts very naturally turned to the treasure I was carrying on me, with nothing but the thin gilt of the pyx between it and my breast. Many times already I had derived joy and sustenance from the fact of this divine presence. But this time a new idea dawned on me, which soon drove out all other preoccupations whether of recollection or of adoration: I suddenly realized just how extraordinary and how disappointing it was to be thus *holding so close to oneself* the wealth of the world and the very source of life *without being able to possess it* inwardly, *without being able either to penetrate it* or to assimilate it. How could Christ be at once so close to my heart and so far from it, so closely united to my body and so remote from my soul?

"I had the feeling that an intangible but invincible barrier separated me from him with whom nevertheless I could hardly be in closer contact since I was holding him in my hands. I fretted at the thought of holding Happiness in a sealed receptacle. I was reminded of a bee buzzing round a pot filled with nectar but tightly closed. And impatiently I pressed the pyx against me, as though this instinctive action could cause Christ to enter more deeply into me. Finally, feeling I could not continue thus any longer, and it being now the hour when I usually said Mass when things were quiet, I opened the pyx and gave myself Holy Communion.

"But now it seemed to me that in the depths of my being, though the Bread I had just eaten had become flesh of my flesh, nevertheless *it remained outside of me.*

"I then summoned to my aid all my powers of recollection. I concentrated on the divine particle, the deepening silence and mounting love of my mind and heart. I made myself limitlessly humble, as docile and tractable as a child, so as not to run counter in any way to the least desires of my heavenly guest but to make myself indistinguishable from him, and through my submission to him, to become one with the members of the physical organism which his soul so completely directed. I went on and on without respite trying to purify my heart so as to make my inmost being ever more transparent to the light which I was sheltering within me.

"Vain yet blessed attempt!

"Still the host seemed to be always ahead of me, always further on in a more complete concentration and opening out of my desires, further on in a greater permeability of my being to the divine influences, further on in a more absolute limpidity of my affective powers. By my withdrawal into myself and my continual purification of my being I was penetrating ever more deeply into it: but I was like a stone that rolls down a precipice without ever reaching the bottom. Tiny though the host was, I was losing myself in it without ever being able to grasp it or to coincide with it: its center was *receding from me as it drew me on.*

"Since I could never reach the inmost depths of the host, it struck me that I might at least manage to grasp it by its whole surface. For that surface was very smooth and very small. I tried therefore to coincide with it externally, to correspond exactly to its contours.

"But there a new infinity awaited me; which dashed my hopes.

"When I tried to envelope the sacred particle in my love, so jealously that I clung to it without losing an atom's breadth of precious content with it, what happened was, in effect, that each touch produced a new differentiation, a new complexity, so that each time I thought to have encompassed it I found that what I was holding was not the host at all but one or other of the thousand entities which make up our lives: a suffering, a joy, a task, a friend to love or to console. . . .

"Thus, in the depths of my heart, through a marvelous substitution, the host was eluding me by means of its own surface, and leaving me at grips with the entire universe which had reconstituted itself and drawn itself forth from its sensible appearances.

"I will not dwell on the feeling of rapture produced in me by this revelation of the universe placed between Christ and myself like a magnificent prey. I will only say, returning to that special impression of "exteriority" which had initiated the vision, that I now understood the nature of the invisible barrier which stood between the pyx and myself. From the host which I held in my fingers I was separated *by the full extent and the density of the years* which still remained to me, to be lived and to be divinized."

"Here my friend hesitated a moment. Then he added:

"I don't know why it is, but for some time now I have had the impression, as I hold the host in my hands, that between it and me there remains only a thin, barely-formed film. . . .

"I had always," he went on, "been by temperament a 'pantheist.' * I had always felt the pantheist's yearnings to be native to me and unarguable; but had never dared give full rein to them because I could not see how to reconcile them with my faith. Now, since these various experiences (and others as well) I can affirm that I have found my interest in my existence inexhaustible, and my peace indestructible.

"I live at the heart of a single, unique Element, the Center of the universe and present in each part of it: personal Love and cosmic Power.

"To attain to him and become merged into his

* Taking "pantheism" in a very real sense, indeed in the etymological sense of the word (*En pasi panta Theos*, i.e., in St Paul's phrase, God "all in all") but at the same time in an absolutely legitimate sense: for if in the last resort Christians become "one with God" this unity is achieved not by way of identification, God *becoming* all things, but by the action—at once differentiating and unifying—of love, God being all *in* all, which latter concept is strictly in accord with Christian orthodoxy. (Author's note.)

life I have before me the entire universe with its noble struggles, its impassioned quests, its myriads of souls to be healed and made perfect. I can and I must throw myself into the thick of human endeavor, and with no stopping for breath. For the more fully I play my part and the more I bring my efforts to bear on the whole surface of reality, the more also will I attain to Christ and cling close to him.

"God, who is eternal Being-in-itself, is, one might say, everywhere in process of formation *for us*.

"And God is also the heart of everything; so much so that the vast setting of the universe might be engulfed or wither away or be taken from me by death without my joy being diminished. Were creation's dust, which is vitalized by a halo of energy and glory, to be swept away, the substantial Reality wherein every perfection is incorruptibly contained and possessed would remain intact: the rays would be drawn back into their Source, and there I should still hold them all in a close embrace.

"This is why even war does not disconcert me. In a few days' time we shall be thrown into battle for the recapture of Douaumont: a grandiose, almost a fantastic exploit which will mark and symbolize a definitive advance of the world in the liberation of souls. And I tell you this: I shall go into this engagement in a religious spirit, with all my soul, borne on by a single great impetus in which I am unable to distinguish where human emotions end and adoration begins.

"And if I am destined not to return from those heights I would like my body to remain there, molded into the clay of the fortifications, like a living cement thrown by God into the stonework of the New City."

Thus my dear friend spoke to me, one October evening: he whose soul was instinctively in communion with the life, the one life, of all reality and whose body rests now, as he wished, somewhere in the wild countryside around Thiaumont.*

Written before the Douaumont engagement (*Nant-le-Grand, October* 14, 1916)

* Thiaumont, a farm near Douaumont. (Ed. note.)

THE SPIRITUAL POWER
OF MATTER

The man was walking in the desert, followed by his companion, when the Thing swooped down on him.

From afar it had appeared to him, quite small, gliding over the sand, no bigger than the palm of a child's hand—as a pale, fleeting shadow like a wavering flight of quail over the blue sea before sunrise or a cloud of gnats dancing in the sun at evening or a whirlwind of dust at midday sweeping over the plain.

The Thing seemed to take no heed of the two travelers, and was roaming capriciously through the wilderness. Then, suddenly, it assumed a set course and with the speed of an arrow came straight at them.

And then the man perceived that the little pale cloud of vapor was but the center of an infinitely greater reality moving towards them without restriction, formless, boundless. The Thing as it approached them spread outwards with prodigious rapidity as far as his eye could reach, filling the whole of space, while its feet brushed lightly over

the thorny vegetation beside the torrent, its brow
rose in the sky like a golden mist with the redden-
ing sun behind it. And all about it the ether had become alive, vibrating palpably beneath the crude
substance of rocks and plants as in summer the
landscape quivers behind the overheated soil in the
foreground.

What was advancing towards them was the *moving heart of an immeasurable pervasive subtlety.*

The man fell prostrate to the ground; and hiding
his face in his hands he waited.

A great silence fell around him.

Then, suddenly, a breath of scorching air passed
across his forehead, broke through the barrier of
his closed eyelids, and penetrated his soul. The
man felt that he was ceasing to be merely himself;
an irresistible rapture took possession of him as
though all the sap of all living things, flowing at
one and the same moment into the too narrow
confines of his heart, was mightily refashioning the
enfeebled fibers of his being. And at the same time
the anguish of some superhuman peril oppressed
him, a confused feeling that the force which had
swept down upon him was equivocal, turbid, the
combined essence of all evil and all goodness.

The hurricane was within himself.

And now, in the very depths of the being it had
invaded, the tempest of life, infinitely gentle, infinitely brutal, was murmuring to the one secret
point in the soul which it had not altogether
demolished:

"You called me: here I am. Driven by the Spirit

far from humanity's caravan routes, you dared to venture into the untouched wilderness; grown weary of abstractions, of attentuations, of the wordiness of social life, you wanted to pit yourself against Reality entire and untamed.

"You had need of me in order to grow; and I was waiting for you in order to be made holy.

"Always you have, without knowing it, desired me; and always I have been drawing you to me.

"And now I am established on you for life, or for death. You can never go back, never return to commonplace gratifications or untroubled worship. He who has once seen me can never forget me: he must either damn himself with me or save me with himself.

"Are you coming?"

"O you who are divine and mighty, what is your name? Speak."

"I am the fire that consumes and the water that overthrows; I am the love that initiates and the truth that passes away. All that compels acceptance and all that brings renewal; all that breaks apart and all that binds together; power, experiment, progress—matter: all this am I.

"Because in my violence I sometimes slay my lovers; because he who touches me never knows what power he is unleashing, wise men fear me and curse me. They speak of me with scorn, calling me beggar-woman or witch or harlot; but their words are at variance with life, and the Pharisees who condemn me, waste away in the outlook to which they confine themselves; they die of inanition and their disciples desert them because I am the essence of all that is tangible, and men cannot do without me.

"You who have grasped that the world—the world beloved of God—has, even more than individuals, a soul to be redeemed,* lay your whole being wide open to my inspiration, and receive the spirit of the earth which is to be saved.

"The supreme key to the enigma, the dazzling utterance which is inscribed on my brow and which henceforth will burn into your eyes even though you close them, is this: *Nothing is precious save what is yourself in others and others in yourself.* In heaven, all things are but one. In heaven all is one.

"Come, do you not feel my breath uprooting you and carrying you away? Up, man of God, and make haste. For according to the way a man surrenders himself to it, the whirlwind will either drag him down into the darkness of its depths or lift him up into the blue skies. Your salvation and mine hang on this first moment."

"O you who are matter: my heart, as you see, is trembling. Since it is you, tell me: what would you have me do?"

"Take up your arms, O Israel, and do battle boldly against me."

The wind, having at first penetrated and pervaded him stealthily, like a philter, had now become aggressive, hostile.

* The soul of the *pleroma*, i.e. of the consummation, in Christ, of the travail of creation; cf. *The Future of Man*, p. 308. (Ed. note.)

From within its coils it exhaled now the acrid stench of battle.

The musky smell of forests, the feverish atmosphere of cities, the sinister, heady scent that rises up from nations locked in battle: all this writhed within its folds, a vapor gathered from the four corners of the earth.

The man, still prostrate, suddenly started, as though his flesh had felt the spur: he leapt to his feet and stood erect, facing the storm.

It was the soul of his entire race that had shuddered within him: an obscure memory of a first sudden awakening in the midst of beasts stronger, better-armed than he; a sad echo of the long struggle to tame the corn and to master the fire; a rancorous dread of the maleficent forces of nature, a lust for knowledge and possession. . . .

A moment ago, in the sweetness of the first contact, he had instinctively longed to lose himself in the warm wind which enfolded him.

Now, this wave of bliss in which he had all but melted away was changed into a ruthless determination towards increased being.

The man had scented the enemy, his hereditary quarry.

He dug his feet into the ground, and began his battle.

He fought first of all in order not to be swept away; but then he began to fight for the joy of fighting, the joy of feeling his own strength. And the longer he fought, the more he felt an increase of strength going out from him to balance the strength of the tempest, and from the tempest there came forth in return a new exhalation which flowed like fire into his veins.

As on certain nights the sea around a swimmer will grow luminous, and its eddies will glisten the more brightly under the sturdy threshing of his limbs, so the dark power wrestling with the man was lit up with a thousand sparkling lights under the impact of his onslaught.

In a reciprocal awakening of their opposed powers, he stirred up his utmost strength to achieve the mastery over it, while it revealed all its treasures in order to surrender them to him.

"Son of earth, steep yourself in the sea of matter, bathe in its fiery waters, for it is the source of your life and your youthfulness.

"You thought you could do without it because the power of thought has been kindled in you? You hoped that the more thoroughly you rejected the tangible, the closer you would be to spirit: that you would be more divine if you lived in the world of pure thought, or at least more angelic if you fled the corporeal? Well, you were like to have perished of hunger.

"You must have oil for your limbs, blood for your veins, water for your soul, the world of reality for your intellect: do you not see that the very law of your own nature makes these a necessity for you?

"Never, if you work to live and to grow, never will you be able to say to matter, "I have seen enough of you; I have surveyed your mysteries and have taken from them enough food for my thought to last me for ever." I tell you: even though, like the Sage of sages, you carried in your memory the image of all the beings that people the earth or swim in the seas, still all that knowledge would be as nothing for your soul, for all abstract knowledge is only a faded reality: this is because to understand the world knowledge is not enough, you must see it, touch it, live in its presence and drink the vital heat of existence in the very heart of reality.

"Never say, then, as some say: "The kingdom of matter is worn out, matter is dead": till the very end of time matter will always remain young, exuberant, sparkling, newborn for those who are willing.

"Never say, 'Matter is accursed, matter is evil': for there has come one who said, 'You will drink poisonous draughts and they shall not harm you,' and again, 'Life shall spring forth out of death,' and then finally, the words which spell my definitive liberation, 'This is my body.'

"Purity does not lie in separation from, but in a deeper penetration into the universe. It is to be found in the love of that unique, boundless Essence which penetrates the inmost depths of all things and there, from within those depths, deeper than the mortal zone where individuals and multitudes struggle, works upon them and molds them. Purity lies in a chaste contact with that which is 'the same in all.'

"Oh, the beauty of spirit as it rises up adorned with all the riches of the earth!

"Son of man, bathe yourself in the ocean of matter; plunge into it where it is deepest and most violent; struggle in its currents and drink of its waters.

For it cradled you long ago in your preconscious existence; and it is that ocean that will raise you up to God."

Standing amidst the tempest, the man turned his head, looking for his companion.

And in that same moment he perceived a strange metamorphosis: the earth was simultaneously vanishing away yet growing in size.

It was vanishing away, for here, immediately beneath him, the meaningless variations in the terrain were diminishing and dissolving; on the other hand it was growing ever greater, for there in the distance the curve of the horizon was climbing ceaselessly higher.

The man saw himself standing in the center of an immense cup, the rim of which was closing over him.

And then the frenzy of battle gave place in his heart to an irresistible longing to *submit:* and in a flash he discovered, everywhere present around him, *the one thing necessary.*

Once and for all he understood that, like the atom, man has no value save for that part of himself which passes into the universe. He recognized with absolute certainty the empty fragility of even the noblest theorizings as compared with the definitive plenitude of the smallest *fact* grasped in its total, concrete reality.

He saw before his eyes, revealed with pitiless clarity, the ridiculous pretentiousness of human claims to order the life of the world, to impose on the world the dogmas, the standards, the conventions of man.

He tasted, sickeningly, the triteness of men's joys and sorrows, the mean egoism of their pursuits, the insipidity of their passions, the attenuation of their power to feel.

He felt pity for those who take fright at the span of a century or whose love is bounded by the frontiers of a nation.

So many things which once had distressed or revolted him—the speeches and pronouncements of the learned, their assertions and their prohibitions, their refusal to allow the universe to move—all seemed to him now merely ridiculous, nonexistent, compared with the majestic reality, the flood of energy, which now revealed itself to him: ominpresent, unalterable in its truth, relentless in its development, untouchable in its serenity, maternal and unfailing in its protectiveness.

Thus at long last he had found a *point d'appui,* he had found refuge, *outside* the confines of human society.

A heavy cloak slipped from his shoulders and fell to the ground behind him: the dead weight of all that is false, narrow, tyrannical, all that is *artificially contrived,* all that is merely *human* in humanity.

A wave of triumph freed his soul.

And he felt that henceforth nothing in the world would ever be able to alienate his heart from the great reality which was now revealing itself to him, nothing at all: neither the intrusiveness and individualist separatism of human beings (for these qualities in them he despised) nor the heavens and the earth in their height and breadth and depth and power (for it was precisely to these that he was now dedicating himself for ever).

A deep process of renewal had taken place within him: now it would never again be possible for him to be human save *on another plane*. Were he to descend again now to the everyday life of earth—even though it were to rejoin his faithful companion, still prostrate over there on the desert sand—he would henceforth be for ever *a stranger*.

Yes, of this he was certain: even for his brothers in God, better men than he, he would inevitably speak henceforth in an incomprehensible tongue, he whom the Lord had drawn to follow the road of fire. Even for those he loved the most his love would be henceforth a burden, for they would sense his compulsion to be for ever seeking something *behind themselves*.

Because matter, throwing off its veil of restless movement and multiplicity, had revealed to him its glorious unity, chaos now divided him from other men. Because it had for ever withdrawn his heart from all that is merely local or individual, all that is fragmentary, henceforth for him it alone in its totality would be his father and mother, his family, his race, his unique, consuming passion.

And not a soul in the world could do anything to change this.

Turning his eyes resolutely away from what was receding from him, he surrendered himself, in super-abounding faith, to the wind which was sweeping the universe onwards.

And now in the heart of the whirling cloud a light was growing, a light in which there was the tenderness and the mobility of a human glance; and from it there spread a warmth which was not now like the harsh heat radiating from a furnace but like the opulent warmth which emanates from a human body. What had been a blind and feral immensity was now becoming expressive and personal; and its hitherto amorphous expanses were being molded into features of an ineffable face.

A Being was taking form in the totality of space; a Being with the attractive power of a soul, palpable like a body, vast as the sky; a Being which mingled with things yet remained distinct from them; a Being of a higher order than the substance of things with which it was adorned, yet taking shape within them.

The rising Sun was being born in the heart of the world.

God was shining forth from the summit of that world of matter whose waves were carrying up to him the world of spirit.

The man fell to his knees in the fiery chariot which was bearing him away.

And he spoke these words:

Hymn to Matter

"Blessed be you, harsh matter, barren soil, stubborn rock: you who yield only to violence, you who force us to work if we would eat.

"Blessed be you, perilous matter, violent sea, untameable passion: you who unless we fetter you will devour us.

"Blessed be you, mighty matter, irresistible march of evolution, reality ever newborn; you who, by constantly shattering our mental categories, force us to go ever further and further in our pursuit of the truth.

"Blessed be you, universal matter, immeasurable time, boundless ether, triple abyss of stars and atoms and generations: you who by overflowing and dissolving our narrow standards or measurement reveal to us the dimensions of God.

"Blessed be you, impenetrable matter: you who, interposed between our minds and the world of essences, cause us to languish with the desire to pierce through the seamless veil of phenomena.

"Blessed be you, mortal matter: you who one day will undergo the process of dissolution within us and will thereby take us forcibly into the very heart of that which exists.

"Without you, without your onslaughts, without your uprootings of us, we should remain all our lives inert, stagnant, puerile, ignorant both of ourselves and of God. You who batter us and then dress our wounds, you who resist us and yield to us, you who wreck and build, you who shackle and liberate, the sap of our souls, the hand of God, the flesh of Christ: it is you, matter, that I bless.

"I bless you, matter, and you I acclaim: not as the pontiffs of science or the moralizing preachers depict you, debased, disfigured—a mass of brute forces and base appetites—but as you reveal yourself to me today, *in your totality and your true nature*.

"You I acclaim as the inexhaustible potentiality for existence and transformation wherein the predestined substance germinates and grows.

"I acclaim you as the universal power which brings together and unites, through which the multitudinous monads are bound together and in which they all converge on the way of the spirit.

"I acclaim you as the melodious fountain of water whence spring the souls of men* and as the limpid crystal whereof is fashioned the new Jerusalem.

"I acclaim you as the divine *milieu*, charged with creative power, as the ocean stirred by the Spirit, as the clay molded and infused with life by the incarnate Word.

"Sometimes, thinking they are responding to your irresistible appeal, men will hurl themselves for love of you into the exterior abyss of selfish pleasure-seeking: they are deceived by a reflection or by an echo.

"This I now understand.

"If we are ever to reach you, matter, we must, having first established contact with the totality of all that lives and moves here below, come little by

* If the work of creation is seen as an evolutionary process, then existence of matter is the necessary precondition for the appearance, on earth, of spirit: elsewhere Père Teilhard de Chardin speaks of matter in more exact language as the "matrix of spirit": that *in* which life emerges and is supported, not the active principle *from* which it takes its rise. (Ed. note.)

little to feel that the individual shapes of all we have laid hold on are melting away in our hands, until finally we are at grips with the *single essence* of all subsistencies and all unions.

"If we are ever to possess you, having taken you rapturously in our arms, we must then go on to sublimate you through sorrow.

"Your realm comprises those serene heights where saints think to avoid you—but where your flesh is so transparent and so agile as to be no longer distinguishable from spirit.

"Raise me up then, matter, to those heights, through struggle and separation and death; raise me up until, at long last, it becomes possible for me in perfect chastity to embrace the universe." *

* It must be made quite clear that he who, not on the fringe of the Christian mystical tradition but at its point of fullest development, was able without imprudence to engage in this formidable battle with matter had prepared himself for it by the most rigorous asceticism: first, in childhood and youth, the asceticism of an unwavering fidelity to the Christian ideal; later, that of a careful and constant obedience to the exigencies of a vocation which would lead him on without respite up the steeply climbing road to perfection till he came to that solitude which he himself described: "he would henceforth be for ever a stranger . . . , he would inevitably speak henceforth in an incomprehensible tongue, he whom the Lord had drawn to follow the road of fire." And elsewhere he wrote: "It seems to me that the point of origin of this invasion and envelopment of my being was the rapidly increasing importance which the sense of *God's will was* assuming in my spiritual life." (*Le Coeur de la Matière*.)

There was need of that long, heroic journey through the mystical dark night, and of an exceptional development of the theological virtues of faith, hope and love, before matter could become "diaphanous" to Père Teilhard's eyes and

Down below on the desert sands, now tranquil again, someone was weeping and calling out: "My Father, my Father! What wild wind can this be that has borne him away?"

And on the ground there lay a cloak.

Jersey, 8th August 1919

---

could reveal to him within itself not only the hallowing stream which flows from the Incarnation and the Eucharist but also the radiant presence of Christ.

For an exact understanding of the *Hymn to Matter*, therefore, we must place it at the end of the way of purgation and looking on and up to the mountaintop where the heavenly Jerusalem shines forth.

It follows that an inexperienced Christian would be making a dangerous mistake if he thought to follow in Père Teilhard's footsteps without first of all treading, like him, the traditional paths of asceticsm. (Ed. note.)

PENSÉES

In cordis
jubilo
Christum
natum
adoremus
cum novo
cantico

THE PRESENCE OF GOD
IN THE WORLD*

1

Let us pray:
Lord Jesus Christ, you truly contain within your
gentleness, within your humanity, all the unyield-
ing immensity and grandeur of the world. And it is
because of this, it is because there exists in you this
ineffable synthesis of what our human thought and
experience would never have dared join together in
order to adore them—element and totality, the one
and the many, mind and matter, the infinite and the
personal; it is because of the indefinable contours
which this complexity gives to your appearance
and to your activity, that my heart, enamoured of
cosmic reality, gives itself passionately to you.

I love you, Lord Jesus, because of the multitude
who shelter within you and whom, if one clings
closely to you, one can hear with all the other
beings murmuring, praying, weeping. . . .

I love you because of the transcendent and inexorable fixity of your purposes, which causes your
gentle friendship to be colored by an intransigent

* Selected by Fernande Tardivel from Père Teilhard's published and unpublished works.

determinism and to gather us all ruthlessly into the folds of its will.

I love you as the source, the activating and life-giving ambience, the term and consummation, of the world, even of the natural world, and of its process of becoming.

You the Center at which all things meet and which stretches out over all things so as to draw them back into itself: I love you for the extensions of your body and soul to the farthest corners of creation through grace, through life, and through matter.

Lord Jesus, you who are as gentle as the human heart, as fiery as the forces of nature, as intimate as life itself, you in whom I can melt away and with whom I must have mastery and freedom: I love you as a world, as *this* world which has captivated my heart;—and it is you, I now realize, that my brother-men, even those who do not believe, sense and seek throughout the magic immensities of the cosmos.

Lord Jesus, you are the center toward which all things are moving: if it be possible, make a place for us all in the company of those elect and holy ones whom your loving care has liberated one by one from the chaos of our present existence and who now are being slowly incorporated into you in the unity of the new earth.

2

The prodigious expanses of time which preceded the first Christmas were not empty of Christ: they

were imbued with the influx of his power. It was
the ferment of his conception that stirred up the
cosmic masses and directed the initial developments of the biosphere. It was the travail preceding
his birth that accelerated the development of instinct and the birth of thought upon the earth. Let
us have done with the stupidity which makes a
stumbling-block of the endless eras of expectancy
imposed on us by the Messiah; the fearful, anonymous labors of primitive man, the beauty fashioned
through its age-long history by ancient Egypt, the
anxious expectancies of Israel, the patient distilling
of the attar of Oriental mysticism, the endless
refining of wisdom by the Greeks: all these were
needed before the Flower could blossom on the rod
of Jesse and of all humanity. All these preparatory
processes were cosmically and biologically necessary that Christ might set foot upon our human
stage. And all this labor was set in motion
by the active, creative awakening of his soul inasmuch as that human soul had been chosen to
breathe life into the universe. When Christ first
appeared before men in the arms of Mary he had
already stirred up the world.

3

Like a river which, as you trace it back to its
source, gradually diminishes till in the end it is lost
altogether in the mud from which it springs, so existence becomes attenuated and finally vanishes
away when we try to divide it up more and more
minutely in space or—what comes to the same—to

drive it further and further back in time. The grandeur of the river is revealed not at its source but at its estuary. In the same way man's secret is to be sought not in the long-outgrown stages of his embryonic life, whether individual or racial, but in the spiritual nature of his soul. Now this soul, whose activity is always a synthesis, in itself eludes the investigations of science, the essential concern of which is to analyze things into their elements and their material antecedents; it can be discovered only by inward vision and philosophic reflection.

Those thinkers are absolutely mistaken, therefore, who imagine they can prove man's nature to be purely material simply by uncovering ever deeper and more numerous roots of his being in the earth. Far from annihilating spirit, they merely show how it mingles with and acts upon the world of matter like a leaven. Let us not play their game by supposing as they do that for a being to come from heaven we must know nothing of the earthly conditions of his origin.

4

When your presence, Lord, has flooded me with its light I hoped that within in it I might find ultimate reality at its most tangible.

But now that I have in fact laid hold on you, you who are utter consistency, and feel myself borne by you, I realize that my deepest hidden desire was not to possess you but to be possessed.

It is not as a radiation of light nor as subtilized matter that I desire you; nor was it thus that I described you in my first intuitive encounter with you: it was as fire. And I can see I shall have no rest unless an active influence, coming forth from you, bears down on me to transform me.

The whole universe is aflame.

Let the starry immensities therefore expand into an ever more prodigious repository of assembled suns;

let the light-rays prolong indefinitely, at each end of the spectrum, the range of their hues and their penetrative power;

let life draw from yet more distant sources the sap which flows through its innumerable branches;

and let us go on and on endlessly increasing our perception of the hidden powers that slumber, and the infinitesimally tiny ones that swarm about us, and the immensities that escape us because they appear to us simply as a point.

From all these discoveries, each of which plunges him a little deeper into the ocean of energy, the mystic derives an unalloyed delight, and his thirst for them is unquenchable; for he will never feel himself sufficiently dominated by the powers of the earth and the skies to be brought under God's yoke as completely as he would wish.

It is in fact God, God alone, who through his Spirit stirs up into a ferment the mass of the universe.

5

A limpid sound rises amidst the silence; a trail of pure color drifts through the glass; a light glows for a moment in the depths of the eyes I love. . . .

Three things, tiny, fugitive: a song, a sunbeam, a glance. . . .

So, at first, I thought they had entered into me in order to remain there and be lost in me.

On the contrary: they took possession of me, and bore me away.

For if this plaint of the air, this tinting of the light, this communication of a soul were so tenuous and so fleeting it was only that they might penetrate the more deeply into my being, might pierce through to that final depth where all the faculties of man are so closely bound together as to become a single point. Through the sharp tips of the three arrows which had pierced me the world itself had invaded my being and had drawn me back into itself.

We imagine that in our sense-perceptions external reality humbly presents itself to us in order to serve us, to help in the building up of our integrity. But this is merely the surface of the mystery of knowledge; the deeper truth is that when the world reveals itself to us it draws us into itself: it causes us to flow outwards into something belonging to it everywhere present in it and more perfect than it.

The man who is wholly taken up with the demands of everyday living or whose *sole* interest is in the outward appearances of things seldom gains more than a glimpse, at best, of this second phase in our sense-perceptions, that in which the world, having entered into us, then withdraws from us and bears us away with it: he can have only a very dim awareness of that aureole, thrilling and inundating our being, through which is disclosed to us at *every* point of contact the unique essence of the universe.

6

Like those materialistic biologists who think they can do away with the soul by dismantling the physico-chemical mechanisms of the living cell, zoologists are persuaded they have done away with the necessity for a first Cause simply because they have discovered a little more about the general structure of his work. It is time we set aside once and for all a problem so invalidly stated. No; strictly speaking, scientific transformism can prove nothing for or against the existence of God. It simply establishes as a fact the concatenation of reality. It offers us an anatomy of life, not an ultimate explanation of life. It affirms that something has become organism, something has developed; but to discern the ultimate conditions of that development is beyond its competence. To decide whether the evolutionary process is self-explanatory or whether it demands for its explanation a progressive and continuous act of creation on the part of a first Mover: this falls within the domain not of physics but of metaphysics.

The theory of transformism, it must be said again and again, does not of itself involve the acceptance of any particular philosophy. Does that mean that it offers no hint in favor of one rather than another? No, indeed. But it is interesting to note that the systems of thought which are best adapted to it would seem to be precisely those which at first regarded it as a menace to them. Christianity, for example, is essentially based on the twofold belief that man is in a special sense an object of pursuit to the divine power throughout creation, and that Christ is the terminal point at which, supernaturally but also physically, the consummation of humanity is destined to be achieved. Could one desire an experiential view of things more in keeping with these doctrines of unity than that which shows us living beings, not artificially set side by side in pursuit of some doubtful utility or amenity, but bound together by virtue of the physical conditions of their existence, in the real unity of a shared struggle towards greater being?

7

Where at first glance we could see only an incoherent arrangement of different altitudes, of landmasses and of waters, there we later established a solid network of real relationships: we animated the earth by communicating to it something of our own unity.

And now, through a gushing forth of vitality in the reverse direction, this life infused by the human mind into the greatest material mass with which we have contact tends to flow back into us under a new guise. When, through our vision of it, we have endowed our earth of iron and stone with "personality," then we find ourselves infected by the desire to build for ourselves in our turn, out of the sum total of all our souls, a spiritual edifice as vast as the one we contemplate, the one brought forth out of the travail of the geogenetic processes. Around the sphere of the earth's rock-mass there stretches a real layer of animated matter, the layer of living creatures and human beings, the biosphere. The great educative value of geology consists in the fact that by disclosing to us an earth which is truly *one*, an earth which is in fact but a single body since it has a face, it recalls to us the possibilities of establishing higher and higher degrees of organic unity in the zone of thought which envelops the world. In truth it is impossible to keep one's gaze constantly fixed on the vast horizons opened out to us by science without feeling the stirrings of an obscure desire to see men drawn closer and closer together by an ever-increasing knowledge and sympathy until finally, in obedience to some divine attraction, there remains but one heart and one soul on the face of the earth.

8

Because of the fundamental unity of the world, every phenomenon, if it is adequately studied even though under one single aspect, reveals itself as being ubiquitous alike in its import and in its roots. Where does this proposition lead us if we apply it to human "self-awareness?"

We might have been tempted to say: "Consciousness manifests itself indubitably only in man; therefore it is an isolated event of no interest to science."

But no, we must correct this, and say rather: "Consciousness manifests itself indubitably in man and therefore, glimpsed in this one flash of light, it reveals itself as having a cosmic extension and consequently as being aureoled by limitless prolongations in space and time."

This conclusion is big with consequences; but I cannot see how it can be denied if sound analogy with all the rest of science is to be preserved.

It is a fact beyond question that deep within ourselves we can discern, as though through a rent, an "interior" at the heart of things; and this glimpse is sufficient to force upon us the conviction that in one degree or another this "interior" exists and has always existed everywhere in nature. Since at one particular point in itself, the stuff of the universe has an inner face, we are forced to conclude that in its very structure—that is, in every region of space and time—it has this double aspect, just as, for instance, in its very structure it is granular. *In all things there is a Within, coextensive with their Without.*

9

Let us ponder over this basic truth till we are steeped in it, till it becomes as familiar to us as our awareness of shapes or our reading of words: God, at his most vitally active and most incarnate, is not remote from us, wholly apart from the sphere of the tangible; on the contrary, at every moment he awaits us in the activity, the work to be done, which every moment brings. He is, in a sense, at the point of my pen, my pick, my paint-brush, my needle—and my heart and my thought. It is by carrying to its natural completion the stroke, the line, the stitch I am working on that I shall lay hold on that ultimate end toward which my will at its deepest levels tends. Like those formidable physical forces which man has so disciplined that they can be made to carry out operations of amazing delicacy, so the enormous might of God's magnetism is brought to bear on our frail desires, our tiny objectives, without ever breaking their point. For it endues us with supervitality; and therefore introduces into our spiritual life a higher principle of unity, the specific effect of which can be seen—according to one's point of view—as either to make human endeavor holy or to make the Christian life fully human.

10

Yes, Lord God, I believe that—and believe all the more readily since it is a question not merely of my being consoled but of my being completed—that it is you who stand at the source of that impulse and at the end point of that magnetic attraction to which all my life long I must be docile, obedient to the initial impulsion and eager to promote its developments. It is you too who quicken for me by your omnipresence—far more effectively than my spirit quickens the matter it animates—the myriad influences which at every moment bear down upon me. In the life springing up within me, in the material elements that sustain me, it is not just your gifts that I discern: it is you yourself that I encounter, you who cause me to share in your own being, and whose hands mold me. In the initial ordering and modulating of the life force which is in me, and in the continuous, helpful action upon me of secondary causes, I am in very truth in contact—and the closest possible contact—with the two aspects of your creative activity; I encounter and I kiss your two wonderful hands: the hand that lays hold on us at so deep a level that it becomes merged, in us, with the sources of life, and the hand whose grasp is so immense that under its slightest pressure all the springs of the universe respond harmoniously together. Of their very nature those blessed passivities which are my will to be, my inclination to be thus or thus, and the chances given me to attain to my own completion in the way I desire, all are charged with your influence—an influence which I shall come before long to see more clearly as the organizing force of your mystical Body. And if I would enter into communion with you in these passivities—a frontal communion, a communion in the sources of life—I have but to recognize you within them and to beg you to be ever more and more fully present in them.

11

The mystic only gradually becomes aware of the faculty he has been given of perceiving the indefinite fringe of reality surrounding the totality of all created things, with more intensity than the precise, individual core of their being.

For a long time, thinking he is the same as other men, he will try to see as they do, to speak their language, to find contentment in the joys with which they are satisfied.

For a long time, seeking to appease his mysterious but obsessive need for plenitude of being, he will try to divert it on to some particularly stable or precious object to which, among all the accessory pleasures of life, he will look for the substance and overflowing richness of his joy.

For a long time he will look to the marvels of art to provide him with that exaltation which will give him access to the sphere—his own sphere—of the extra-personal and the suprasensible; and in the unknown Word of nature he will strive to hear the heartbeats of that higher reality which calls him by name.

Happy the man who fails to stifle his vision.

Happy the man who will not shrink from a passionate questioning of the Muses and of Cybele concerning his God.

But happy above all he who, rising beyond esthetic dilettantism and the materialism of the lower layers of life, is given to hear the reply of all beings, singly and all together: "What you saw gliding past, like a world, behind the song and behind the color and behind the eyes' glance does not exist just here or there but is a Presence existing equally everywhere: a presence which, though it now seems vague to your feeble sight, will grow in clarity and depth. In this presence all diversities and all impurities yearn to be melted away."

12

For Christian humanism—faithful in this to the most firmly established theology of the Incarnation —there is no real independence or discordance but a logical subordination between the genesis of humanity in the world and the genesis of Christ, through his Church, in humanity. Inevitably the two processes are structurally linked together, the second needing the first as the material on which it rests in order to supervitalize it. This point of view fully respects the progressive experimental concentration of human thought in a more and more lively awareness of its unifying role; but in place of the undefined point of convergence required as term for this evolution it is the clearly defined personal reality of the incarnate Word that is made manifest to us and established for us as our objective, that Word "in whom all things subsist."

Life for Man: Man for Christ: Christ for God.

And to ensure the psychic continuity of this vast development in all its phases, extending to the myriads of elements scattered through the immensities of all the ages, there is but one mechanism: education.

Thus all the lines converge, complete one another, interlock. All things are now but one.

13

Without any doubt there is *something* which links material energy and spiritual energy together and makes them a continuity. In the last resort there must *somehow* be but one single energy active in the world. And the first idea that suggests itself to us is that the soul must be a center of transformation at which, through all the channels of nature, corporeal energies come together in order to attain inwardness and be sublimated in beauty and in truth.

But however attractive at first sight we may find this idea of a *direct* transformation of one of the two types of energy into the other, a moment's inspection will force us to abandon it. For as soon as we try to couple them together their independence of one another becomes as evident as their interconnection.

"To think, we must eat." Yes, but what diverse thoughts may spring from the same crust of bread! Just as the same letters of an alphabet can be turned either into nonsense or into the most beautiful of poems, so the same calories seem as indifferent as they are necessary to the spiritual values they nourish.

14

What would become of our souls, Lord, if they lacked the bread of earthly reality to nourish them, the wine of created beauty to intoxicate them, the discipline of human struggle to make them strong? What puny powers and bloodless hearts your creatures would bring to you were they to cut themselves off *prematurely* from the providential setting in which you have placed them! Show us, Lord, how to contemplate the Sphinx without being beguiled into error; how to grasp the mystery hidden here on earth in the womb of death, not by refinements of human learning but in the simple concrete act of your redemptive immersion in matter. Through the sufferings of your incarnate life reveal to us, and then teach us to harness jealousy for you, the spiritual power of matter.

15

Like those translucent materials which can be wholly illumined by a light enclosed within them, the world manifests itself to the Christian mystic as bathed in an inward light which brings out its structure, its relief, its depths. This light is not the superficial coloring that a crude hedonism might discern; nor is it the violent glare that annihilates objects and blinds the eyes; it is the tranquil, mighty radiance born of the synthesis, in Jesus, of all the elements of the world. The more completely the beings thus illumined attain to their natural fulfillment, the closer and more perceptible this radiance will be; and on the other hand the more perceptible it becomes, the more clearly the contours of the objects which it bathes will stand out and the deeper will be their roots.

16

If one considers, however briefly, what conditions will make possible the flowering in the human heart of this new universal love, so often vainly dreamed of but now at last leaving the realm of the utopian and declaring itself as both possible and necessary, one notices this: that if men on earth, all over the earth, are ever to love one another it is not enough for them to recognize in one another the elements of a single *something;* they must also, by developing a "planetary" consciousness, become aware of the fact that without loss of their individual identities they are becoming a single *somebody.* For there is no total love—and this is writ large in the gospel—save that which is in and of the personal.

And what does this mean if not that, in the last resort, the "planetization" of humanity presupposes for its proper development not only the contracting of the earth, not only the organizing and condensing of human thought, but also a *third* factor: the rising on our inward horizon of some psychic cosmic center, some supreme pole of consciousness, towards which all the elementary consciousnesses of the world shall converge and in which they shall be able to love one another: in other words, the rising *of a God.*

17

At every moment the vast and horrible Thing breaks in upon us through the crevices and invades our precarious dwelling place, that Thing we try so hard to forget but which is always there, separated from us only by thin dividing walls: fire, pestilence, earthquake, storm, the unleashing of dark moral forces, all these sweep away ruthlessly, in an instant, what we had labored with mind and heart to build up and make beautiful.

Lord God, my dignity as a man forbids me to shut my eyes to this, like an animal or a child; therefore, lest I succumb to the temptation to curse the universe, and the Maker of the universe, *teach me to adore it by seeing you hidden within it*. Say once again to me, Lord, those great and liberating words, the words which are at once revealing light and effective power: *hoc est Corpus meum*.* In very truth, if only we will it to be so, the immense and somber Thing, the specter, the tempest—is you. *Ego sum, nolite timere*.** All the things in life that fill us with dread, all that filled your own heart with dismay in the garden of agony: all, in the last resort, are the species or appearances, the matter, of one and the same sacrament.

We have only to believe; and to believe all the more firmly, all the more desperately, as the fearful reality which confronts us appears more menacing and more invincible. For then, little by little, we shall see the universal horror lose something of its rigidity, and begin to smile upon us, and finally gather us into its super-human arms.

It is not the rigidity of material or mathematical determinisms that gives the universe its consistency, but the supple orderings of spirit. To those who believe, the innumerable accidents of chance,

* "This is my Body." (Matt. 26.26; Mark 14.22.)

** "It is I, fear not." (Luke 24.36.)

the boundless blindness of the world, are but illusion: *fides substantia rerum.**

18

Lord, it is you who, through the imperceptible goadings of sense beauty, penetrated my heart in order to make its life flow out into yourself. You came down into me by means of a tiny scrap of created reality; and then, suddenly, you unfurled your immensity before my eyes and displayed yourself to me as Universal Being.

So the basic mystical intuition issues in the discovery of a suprareal unity diffused throughout the immensity of the world.

In that *milieu*, at once divine and cosmic, in which he had at first observed only a simplification and as it were a spiritualization of space, the seer, faithful to the light given him, now perceives the gradual delineation of the form and attributes of an ultimate *element* in which all things find their definitive consistency.

And then he begins to measure more exactly the joys, and the pressing demands, of that mysterious presence to which he has surrendered himself.

19

Give me to recognize in other men, Lord God, the radiance of your own face. The irresistible light of

* "Faith is the substance of things to be hoped for." (Heb. 11.1.)

your eyes, shining in the depths of things, has already driven me into undertaking the work I had to do and facing the difficulties I had to overcome: grant me now to see you also and above all in the most inward, most perfect, most remote levels of the souls of my brother-men.

The gift you ask of me for these brothers of mine—the only gift my heart can give them—is not the overflowing tenderness of those special, preferential loves which you implant in our lives as the most powerful created agent of our inward growth: it is something less tender but just as real and of even greater strength. Your will is that, with the help of your Eucharist, between men and my brother-men there should be revealed that basic attraction (already dimly felt in every love once it becomes strong) which mystically transforms the myriads of rational creatures into (as it were) a single monad in you, Christ Jesus.

HUMANITY IN PROGRESS

20

The world is abuilding. This is the basic truth which must first be understood so thoroughly that it becomes an habitual and as it were natural springboard for our thinking. At first sight, beings and their destinies might seem to us to be scattered haphazard or at least in an arbitrary fashion over the face of the earth; we could very easily suppose that each of us might *equally well* have been born

earlier or later, at this place or that, happier or more
ill-starred, as though the universe from the beginning to end of its history formed in space-time a
sort of vast flowerbed in which the flowers could be
changed about at the whim of the gardener. But
this idea is surely untenable. The more one reflects,
with the help of all that science, philosophy and religion can teach us, each in its own field, the more
one comes to realize that the world should be lik-
ened not to a bundle of elements artificially held
together but rather to some organic system animated by a broad movement of development which
is proper to itself. As the centuries go by it seems
that a comprehensive plan is indeed being slowly
carried out around us. A process is at work in the
universe, an issue is at stake, which can best be
compared to the processes of gestation and birth;
the birth of that spiritual reality which is formed
by souls and by such material reality as their
existence involves. Laboriously, through and thanks
to the activity of mankind, the new earth is being
formed and purified and is taking on definition and
clarity. No, we are not like the cut flowers that
make up a bouquet: we are like the leaves and
buds of a great tree on which everything appears at
its proper time and place as required and determined by the good of the whole.

21

Human suffering, the sum total of suffering poured
out at each moment over the whole earth, is like an
immeasurable ocean. But what makes up this im-

mensity? Is it blackness, emptiness, barren wastes? No, indeed: it is potential *energy*. Suffering holds hidden within it, in extreme intensity, the ascensional force of the world. The whole point is to set this force free by making it conscious of what it signifies and of what it is capable. For if all the sick people in the world were simultaneously to turn their sufferings into a single shared longing for the speedy completion of the kingdom of God through the conquering and organizing of the earth, what a vast leap towards God the world would thereby make! If all those who suffer in the world were to unite their sufferings so that the pain of the world should become one single grand act of consciousness, of sublimation, of unification, would not this be one of the most exalted forms in which the mysterious work of creation could be manifested to our eyes?

22

Lord, that I might hold to you the more closely, I would that my consciousness were as wide as the skies and the earth and the peoples of the earth; as deep as the past, the desert, the ocean; as tenuous as the atoms of matter or the thoughts of the human heart.

Must I not adhere to you everywhere throughout the entire extent of the universe?

In order that I may not succumb to the temptation that lies in wait for every act of boldness, nor ever forget that you alone must be sought in and through everything, I know, Lord, that you will send me—at what moments only you know—deprivations, disappointments, sorrow. The object of my love will fall away from me, or I shall outgrow it.

The flower I held in my hands withered in my hands. . . .

At the turn of the lane the wall rose up before me. . . .

Suddenly between the trees I saw the end of the forest which I thought had no end. . . .

The testing-time had come . . .

. . . But it did not bring me unalleviated sorrow. On the contrary, a glorious, unsuspected joy invaded my soul: because, in the collapse of those immediate supports I had risked giving to my life, I knew with a unique experiential certainty that I would never again rely for support on anything save your own divine stability.

23

The development in our souls of *supernatural* life (based on the *natural* spiritualization of the world through the efforts of mankind): this in the last resort is the field where the operative power of faith is positively and without any known limits exercised.

Within the universe it is spirit, and within spirit it is the *moral* sphere, that are *par excellence* the *actual subjects* of the development of life. Consequently it is there, on that plastic center of ourselves where divine grace mingles with earthly drives, that the power of faith should be brought vigorously to bear.

There above all, surely, creative energy awaits us, ready to work in us a transformation beyond anything that human eye has seen or ear heard. Who can say what God would fashion out of us if, trusting in his word, we dared to follow his counsels to the very end and surrender ourselves to his providence?

Let us then, for love of our Creator and of the universe, throw ourselves fearlessly into the crucible of the world of tomorrow.

In brief, there are three characteristics of the Christian fulfillment of this process of life development, brought about by faith:

first, it is effected without any distortion or disruption of any particular determinism: for events are not, in general, deflected from their course of prayer but are integrated into a new arrangement of the totality of forces;

secondly, it is manifested, not necessarily on the plane of natural human achievement, but in the order of supernatural growth to holiness;

thirdly, in real fact it has God as at once its principal agent, its source and its *milieu*.

With this triple reservation, which marks it off clearly from natural faith in its mode of operation, Christian faith can be said to manifest itself as, in the most realistic and comprehensive sense, a "cosmic energy."

24

Within a universe which is structurally convergent the only possible way for one element to draw closer to other, neighboring elements is by *condensing the cone:* that is, by driving towards the point of convergence the whole area of the world in which it is involved. In such a system it is impossible to love one's neighbor without drawing close to God—and *vice versa* for that matter. This we know well enough. But it is also impossible—and this is less familiar to us—to love either God or our neighbor without being obliged to help in the progress of the earthly synthesis of spirit in its physical totality, for it is precisely the advances made in this movement of synthesis that permit us to draw close to one another and at the same time raise us up towards God. Thus, because we love, and in order to love more, we find ourselves happily reduced to sharing—we more and better than anyone—in all the struggles, all the anxieties, all the aspirations, and also all the affections, of the earth *in so far as all these contain within them a principle of ascension and synthesis.*

This breadth of outlook does not involve any modification whatsoever of Christian poverty of spirit.* But instead of "leaving things behind" it carries them onwards; instead of cutting down it raises up: it is a question now not of a breaking away but of a crossing over, not a flight but an emergence. Without ceasing to be itself, charity enlarges its scope to become an upward-lifting force, a common essence, at the heart of every form

---

* I have used this phrase to translate *détachement* in order to avoid the infelicitous and possibly gravely misleading overtones (suggestive of the "couldn't care less" attitude) of "detachment."

of human endeavor, whose diversity tends in consequence to be drawn together in synthesis into the rich totality of a single operation. Like Christ himself and in imitation of him it becomes *universal*, *dynamic* and, for that very reason, fully *human*.

In short, in order to correspond to the new curve of the flow, Christianity is led to the discovery, *below God*, of earthly values, while humanism is led to the discovery, *above the world*, of the place of a God.

25

Joy is above all the fruit of having come face to face with a universal and enduring reality to which one can refer and as it were attach those fragmentary moments of happiness that, being successive and fugitive, excite the heart without satisfying it. The mystic suffers more than other men from the tendency of created things to crumble into dust: instinctively and obstinately he searches for the stable, the unfailing, the absolute . . .

This crumbling away, which is the mark of the corruptible and the precarious, is to be seen everywhere. And yet everywhere there are traces of, and a yearning for, a unique support, a unique and absolute soul, a unique reality in which other realities are brought together in synthesis, as stable and universal as matter, as simple as spirit.

One must have felt deeply the pain of being plunged into that multiplicity which swirls about one and slips through one's fingers if one is to be worthy of experiencing the rapture that transports the soul when, through the influence of the universal Presence, it perceives that reality has become not merely transparent but solidly *enduring*. For this means that the incorruptible principle of the universe is now and for ever found, and that it extends everywhere: *the world is filled,* and filled with the Absolute. To see this is to be made free.

26

*Mane nobiscum Domine, quoniam advesperascit.**

Assimilate, utilize, the *shadows* of later life: enfeeblement, loneliness, the sense that no further horizons lie ahead. . . .

Discover in Christ-Omega** how to remain *young:* gay, enthusiastic, full of enterprise.

Beware of thinking that every form of melancholy, indifference, disenchantment is to be identified with wisdom.

Make a place, and an *upward-lifting* place, for the end which now draws near and for the decline of one's powers to whatever degree God may will.

"To be ready" has never seemed to mean anything to me but this: "To be straining forwards."

* "Stay with us, because it is towards evening." (Luke 24.29.)

** Omega: the end-point of cosmogenesis, the culmination of the process of *hominization* or spiritualization, where personal and universal meet in the Supra-Personal—a point therefore which is not simply the end of the whole process, the last term in its series, but is outside all series, autonomous and transcendent, and so is identified with God, the Center of centers, and with the *Totus Christus.* (Tr. note.)

May Christ-Omega keep me always *young—ad majorem Dei gloriam.*[*] (And what better argument for Christianity could there be than an enduring youthfulness drawn from Christ-Omega?)
For

old age comes from him,

old age leads on to him, and

old age will touch me only in so far as he wills.

To be "young" means to be hopeful, energetic, smiling—and clear-sighted.

Accept death in whatever guise it may come to me in Christ-Omega, that is, within the process of the development of life.

A smile (inward and outward) means facing with sweetness and gentleness whatever befalls one.

Jesus-Omega, grant me to *serve you,* to proclaim you, to glorify you, to make you manifest, to the very end, through all the time that remains to me of life, and above all through my death.

Desperately, Lord Jesus, I commit to your care my last active years, and my death: do not let them impair or spoil the work I have so dreamed of achieving for you.

The grace to end well, in the way that will best advance the glory of Christ-Omega: this is the grace of graces.

Live under the exclusive dominance of a single passion: the impassioned desire to help forward the synthesis of Christ and the universe. This implies

---

[*] "To the greater glory of God."

love of both, and more especially love of the supreme axis, Christ and the Church.

Communion in and through death: to die a communion-death. . . .

What comes to one at the very end: the adorable. I go forward to meet him who comes.

27

Many people suppose that the superiority of spirit would be jeopardized if its first manifestation were not accompanied by some interruption of the normal advance of the world. One ought rather to say that precisely because it is spirit its appearance must take the form of a crowning achievement, or a blossoming. But leaving aside all thought of systematization, is it not true that every day a multitude of human souls are created in the course of an embryogenic process in which scientific observation will never be able to detect any break however small in the chain of biological phenomena? Thus we have daily before our eyes an example of an act of creation which is absolutely imperceptible to, and beyond the reach of, science as such. Why then make so many difficulties when it is a question of the first man? Obviously it is much more difficult for us to imagine the first appearance of reflective thought at some point in the history of a phylum or race made up of different individuals than at some point in the series of states making up the life of one and the same embryo. But from the viewpoint of creative activity considered in relationship to phenomena, ontogenesis and phylogenesis are in like case. Why not admit, for example, that the absolutely free and special act whereby the Creator willed humanity to be the crown of his work so profoundly influenced and organized beforehand the progress of the world prior to man's coming that now this coming seems to us, in accordance with the Creator's choice, to be the natural outcome of all the precedent processes of life-development? *Omnia propter hominem.**

28

If, on the tree of life, the mammals form a dominant branch, indeed *the* dominant branch, then the primates (that is, the cerebro-mammals) are its leading shoot, and the anthropoids are the bud in which the shoot ends.

Hence, we may go on to say, it is easy for us to judge at what point in the biosphere we must fix our gaze in expectation of what is yet to come. Everywhere, as we are well aware, the lines of active phyletic development grow warm with consciousness as they approach the summit; but in one clearly-marked region at the center of the kingdom of mammals, where the most powerful brains ever fashioned by nature are to be found, the lines glow red-hot; and already at the heart of this region there burns a point of incandescence.

It is this line that we must always hold in our gaze, this line glowing crimson with the dawn light.

* "All things are for man's sake."

The flame that for thousands of years has been rising up below the horizon is now, at a strictly localized point, about to burst forth: thought has been born.

29

Beings endowed with self-awareness become, precisely in virtue of that bending back upon themselves, immediately capable of rising into a new sphere of existence: in truth another world is born. Abstract thought, logic, reasoned choice and invention, mathematics, art, the exact computation of space and time, the dreams and anxieties of love: all these activities of the inner life are simply the bubbling up of the newly formed life-center as it explodes upon itself.

This being said, a question arises. If it is in fact the attainment of "self-consciousness" that constitutes true "intelligence," can we seriously doubt that intelligence is the evolutionary prerogative of man alone? And, if it is, can we allow some sort of false modesty to hinder us from recognizing that man's possession of it shows him as representing a radical advance on all precedent forms of life? Certainly animals know; but equally certainly *they cannot know that they know:* otherwise they would long since have multiplied inventions and developed a system of internal constructions which could not have escaped our observation. Hence a whole domain of reality is closed to them, beyond all possibility of access: a domain in which we for our part can move about freely. They are separated from us by an abyss—or a threshold—which they can never cross. Reflective consciousness makes us not merely different from them but wholly other: it is a difference not merely of degree but of kind: a change of nature, resulting from a change of state.

And so we reach precisely the conclusion we had anticipated: since the development of life means the rise and growth of consciousness, that development could not continue indefinitely along its own line without a transformation in depth: like all great developments in the world, life had to become different in order to remain itself.

30

It was a joy to me, Lord, in the midst of my struggles, to feel that in growing to my own fulfillment I was increasing your hold on me; it was a joy to me, beneath the inward burgeoning of life and amidst the unfolding of events that favored me, to surrender myself to your providence. And now that I have discovered the joy of turning every increase into a way of making—or allowing—your presence to grow within me, I beg of you: bring me to a serene acceptance of that final phase of communion with you in which I shall attain to possession of you by diminishing within you.

Now that I have learnt to see you as he who is "more me than myself," grant that *when my hour has come* I may recognize you under the appearances of every alien or hostile power that seems bent on destroying or dispossessing me. When the erosions of age begin to leave their mark on my body, and still more on my mind; when the ills that must diminish my life or put an end to it strike me down from without or grow up from within me; when I reach that painful moment at which I suddenly realize that I am a sick man or that I am growing old; above all at that final moment when I feel I am losing hold on myself and becoming wholly passive in the hands of those great unknown forces which first formed me: at all these somber moments grant me, Lord, to understand that it is you (provided my faith is strong enough) who are painfully separating the fibers of my being so as to penetrate to the very marrow of my substance and draw me into yourself.

The more deeply and incurably my ills become engrained in my flesh, the more it may be you yourself that I am harboring as a loving, active principle of purification and of liberation from possessiveness. The more the future lies ahead of me like a dark tunnel or a dizzy abyss, the more confident I can be—if I go forward boldly, relying on your word—of being lost, of being engulfed, in you, Lord, of being absorbed into your Body.

Lord Christ, you who are divine energy and living, irresistible might: since of the two of us it is you who are infinitely the stronger, it is you who must set me ablaze and transmute me into fire that we may be welded together and made one. Grant me, then, something even more precious than that grace for which all your faithful followers pray: to receive communion as I die is not sufficient: *teach me to make a communion of death itself.*

31

No mechanism of evolution could gain a hold on an entirely passive (or *a fortiori* resistant) cosmic material. Hence we cannot fail to see the drama inherent in the possibility that mankind might suddenly lose all desire to achieve its destiny. Such a disenchantment would be conceivable, would indeed be inevitable, if as a result of increasing reflection we came to see that in a hermetically closed world we were destined one day to end up in a total collective death. In the face of this terrifying fact, is it not clear that despite the most violent pull from the winding-chain of planetary development the psychic mechanism of evolution would come to a dead stop, its very substance stretched to breaking point and finally disintegrating?

The more one reflects on this eventuality—and certain morbid symptoms such as the existentialism of Sartre prove that it is no mere fantasy—the more one comes to the conclusion that the great enigma presented to our minds by the phenomenon of man is not so much how life could ever have been kindled on earth as how it could ever be extinguished on earth without finding some continuance elsewhere. For once life has become reflective consciousness it cannot in fact accept utter extinction without biologically contradicting itself.

Consequently one feels less inclined to reject as unscientific the idea that the critical point of planetary reflective consciousness which is the result of the forming of humanity into an organized society, far from being a mere spark in the darkness, corre-

sponds on the contrary to our passage (by a movement of reversal or dematerialization) to another
face of the universe: not an ending of the ultrahu-
man but its arrival at something transhuman at the
very heart of reality.

32

For one who sees the universe in the guise of a laborious communal ascent towards the summit of
consciousness, life, far from seeming blind, hard or
despicable, becomes charged with gravity, with
responsibilities, with new relationships. Sir Oliver
Lodge very justly remarked not so long ago that,
properly understood, the doctrine of evolution is a
"school of hope"—and, let us add, a school of ever
greater mutual charity and ever greater effort.

So much so that all along the line one can up-
hold, and without paradox, the following thesis
(which is doubtless the one best calculated to reas-
sure and guide men's minds when confronted with
the growth of transformist views): transformism
does not necessarily open the way to an invasion of
spirit by matter; rather does it give evidence in
favor of an essential triumph of spirit. Transformism as well as, if not better than, the theory of
"fixed types" can give to the universe that grandeur
and depth and unity which are the natural atmosphere for Christian faith.

And this last consideration leads us to formulate
the following general conclusion:

whatever we Christians may say in the last resort
about transformism or about any other of the new

theories which attract the modern mind, let us never give the impression of being timid about anything that can bring fresh light and greater breadth to our ideas concerning man and the universe. The world will never be vast enough, nor humanity powerful enough, to be worthy of him who created them and is incarnate in them.

33

Is life an open road or a blind alley? This question, barely formulated a few centuries ago, is today explicitly on the lips of mankind as a whole. As a result of the brief, violent moment of crisis in which it became conscious at once of its creative power and of its critical faculties, humanity has quite legitimately become hard to move: no stimulus at the level of mere instinct or blind economic necessity will suffice for long to goad it into moving onwards. Only a reason, and a valid and important reason, for loving life passionately will cause it to advance further. But where, at the experiential level, are we to find, if not a complete justification, at least the beginnings of a justification of life? Only, it would seem, in the consideration of the intrinsic value of the phenomenon of man. Continue to regard man as an accidental outgrowth or sport of nature and you will drive him into a state of disgust or revolt which, if it became general, would mean the definitive stoppage of life on earth. Recognize, on the other hand, that within the domain of our experience man is at the head of one of the two greatest waves into which, for us, tangible reality is divided, and that therefore he holds in his hands the fortunes of the universe: and immediately you cause him to turn his face towards the grandeur of a new sunrise.

Man has every right to be anxious about his fate so long as he feels himself to be lost and lonely in the midst of the mass of created things. But let him once discover that his fate is bound up with the fate of nature itself, and immediately, joyously, he will begin again his forward march. For it would denote in him not a critical sense but a malady of the spirit if he were doubtful of the value and the hopes of an entire world.

34

It is easy for the pessimist to belittle that extraordinary period of history during which in the space of a few thousand years civilizations crumbled one after another into ruin. But it is surely far more scientific to discern once again, beneath these successive waxings and wanings, the great spiral of life always irreversibly ascending, but by stages, along the dominant line of its evolution. Susa, Memphis, Athens may crumble: but an ever more highly organized awareness of the universe is passed on from hand to hand and increases with each successive stage in clarity and brilliance.

When we are dealing in general with the gradual development of the noosphere into planetary consciousness we must of course do full justice to the great, the essential part played by the other sections of the human race in bringing about the

eventual plenitude of the earth. But in dealing
with this historical period we should be allowing
sentiment to falsify fact if we refused to recognize
that during its centuries the principal axis of an-
thropogenesis has passed through the West. It was
in this ardent zone of growth and universal recast-
ing that all that makes man what he is today was
discovered—or at least *must have been rediscov-
ered,* for even those things which had long been
known elsewhere achieved their definitive human
value only when they were incorporated into the
system of European ideas and activities. We are
not being merely naïve if we hail as a great event
the discovery by Columbus of America.

The fact is that during the last six thousand
years, in the Mediterranean area, a neohumanity
has been germinating and is now at this moment
completing its absorption into itself of the remaining vestiges of the neolithic mosaic of ethnic
groupings, so as to form a new layer, of greater
density than all the others, on the noosphere.

And the proof of this is that today, in order to remain human or to become more fully human, all
the peoples from end to end of the earth are being
inexorably led to formulate the world's hopes and
problems in the very terms devised by the West.

35

Let us admit this frankly, once and for all: what
most discredits faith in progress in the eyes of men
today, over and above its reticences and its help-
lessness in meeting the cry of the "last days of the

human species," is the unfortunate tendency still shown by its adepts to distort into pitiful millenarianisms all that is most valid and most noble in our now permanently awakened expectation of the future appearance of some form of "ultrahumanity." An era of abundance and euphoria—a Golden Age —is, they suggest, all that evolution could hold in reserve for us. And it is but right that our hearts should sink at the thought of so "bourgeois" an ideal.

In face of this strictly "pagan" materialism and naturalism it becomes a pressing duty to remind ourselves once again that, if the laws of biogenesis of their nature suppose and effectively bring about an economic improvement in human living conditions, it is not any question of *well-being*, it is solely a thirst for *greater being* that by psychological necessity can save the thinking world from the *taedium vitae*.

And here we can see with complete clarity the importance of the idea, suggested above, that it is at its point or superstructure of spiritual concentration and not at its base or infrastructure of material arrangement that humanity must biologically establish its equilibrium.

For once we admit, following this life of argument, the existence of a *critical point of species-formation** at the end of the evolution of technical developments and civilizations, we realize that what finally opens out at the peak of time (maintaining to the end the priority of tension over rest

* Fr. *spéciation*. (Tr. note.)

in biogenesis) is an *issue:* an issue not merely for our hopes of escape but also for our awaiting of some revelation.

And this is exactly what could best relieve that tension between light and darkness, exaltation and anguish, into which a renewed awareness of our human species has plunged us.

36

Fold your wings, my soul, those wings you had spread wide to soar to the terrestrial peaks where the light is most ardent: it is for you simply to await the descent of the Fire—supposing it to be willing to take possession of you.

If you would attract its power to yourself you must first loosen the bonds of affection which still tie you to objects cherished too exclusively for their own sake. The true union you ought to seek with creatures that attract you is to be found not by going directly to them but by converging with them on God sought in and through them. It is not by making themselves more material, relying solely on physical contacts, but by making themselves more spiritual in the embrace of God that things draw closer to each other and, following their invincible natural bent, end by becoming, all of them together, one. Therefore, my soul, be chaste.

And when you have thus refined your crude materiality you must loosen yet further the fibers of your substance. In your excessive self-love you are like a molecule closed in upon itself and incapable of entering easily into any new grouping. God looks to you to be more open and more pliant. If you are to enter into him you need to be freer and more eager. Have done then with your egoism and your fear of suffering. Love others as you love yourself, that is to say admit them into yourself, all of them, even those whom, if you were a pagan, you would exclude. Accept pain. Take up your cross, my soul. . . .

37

We always tend to forget that the supernatural is a leaven, a life-principle, not a complete organism. Its purpose is to transform "nature"; and it cannot do that apart from the material with which nature presents it. If the Hebrews kept their gaze fixed for three thousand years on the coming of the Messiah it was because they saw him effulgent with the glory of their own people. If St Paul's disciples lived in a constant eager yearning for the great day of the second coming of Christ it was because they looked to the Son of Man to give them a personal, tangible solution to the problems and the injustices of earthly life. The expectation of heaven cannot be kept alive unless it is made flesh. With what body, then, shall our own be clothed?

With an immense, *completely human* hope.

38

You whose loving wisdom fashions my being out of all the forces and all the hazards of earth, teach me to adopt here and now, however clumsily, an attitude the full efficacy of which will be plain to me when I am face to face with the powers of diminishment and death: grant that having desired I may believe, and believe ardently, believe above all things, in your active presence.

Thanks to you, this faith and this expectancy are already full of effective power. But how am I to show you, and prove to myself, through some visible endeavor, that I am not of those who, with their lips only, cry to you "Lord, Lord"? I shall cooperate with that divine power through which you act upon me and anticipate my initiatives; and I shall do so in two ways.

First, to that profound inspiration whereby you impel me to seek the fullness of being I shall respond by striving never to stifle or distort or squander my powers of loving and making. And then, to your all-embracing providence which at each moment shows me, through the events of the day, the next step I must take, the next rung I must climb, I shall respond by striving never to miss an opportunity of rising up towards the realm of spirit.

39

"O ye of little faith," why fear or hold aloof from the onward march of the world? Why foolishly multiply your prophecies of woe and your prohibitions: "Don't venture there; don't attempt that; everything is already known that can be known; the earth is grown old and stale and empty; there is nothing more for us to find. . . ."

On the contrary, we must try everything for

Christ; we must hope everything for Christ. *Nihil
intentatum:*° that is the true Christian attitude.
Divinization means not destruction but supercrea-
tion. We can never know all that the Incarnation
still asks of the world's potentialities. We can never
hope for too much from the growing unity of mankind.

THE MEANING OF
HUMAN ENDEAVOR

40

The aspect of life which most stirs my soul is the
ability to share in an undertaking, in a reality, more
enduring than myself: it is in this spirit and with
this purpose in view that I try to perfect myself
and to master things a little more. When death lays
its hand upon me it will leave intact these things,
these ideas, these realities which are more solid and
more precious than I; moreover, my faith in Providence makes me believe that death comes at its
own fixed moment, a moment of mysterious and
special fruitfulness not only for the supernatural
destiny of the soul but also for the further progress
of the earth. Why then should I be afraid or filled
with grief, if the essential thing in my life remains
untouched, if the pattern will not be broken off but
will be extended further without any harmful interruption of continuity? The realities of faith cannot
give us the same *feeling* of solidity as those of expe-

° "To leave nothing unattempted."

rience; hence, inevitably and providentially, when
we have to leave these for those we feel terrified
and bewildered: but that is the very moment at
which we must ensure the triumph of adoration
and trust and the joy of being part of a totality
greater than ourselves.

41

In the lowliness of fear and the thrill of danger we
carry on the work of completing an element which
the mystical body of Christ can draw *only* from us.
Thus to our peace is added the exaltation of creat-
ing, perilously, an eternal work which will not exist
without us. Our trust in God is quickened and
made firmer by the passionate eagerness of man to
conquer the earth.

42

It would be surprising to find, in a bouquet, flowers
which were ill-formed or sickly, since these flowers
are picked one by one and artificially grouped together in a bunch. But on a tree which has had to
struggle against inner accidents of its own development and external accidents of climate, the broken
branches, the torn leaves, and the dried or sickly or
wilted blossoms have their place: they reveal to us
the greater or lesser difficulties encountered by the
tree itself in its growth.

Similarly in a universe where each creature
formed a little enclosed unit, designed simply for
its own sake and theoretically transposable at will,

we should find some difficulty in justifying in our own minds the presence of individuals whose potentialities and upward-soaring drives had been painfully impeded. Why this gratuitous inequality, these gratuitous frustrations?

If on the other hand the world is in truth a battlefield whereon victory is in the making—and if we are in truth thrown at birth into the thick of the battle—then we can at least vaguely see how, for the success of this universal struggle in which we are both fighters and the issue at stake, there must inevitably be suffering. Seen from the viewpoint of our human experience and drawn to our human scale, the world appears as an immense groping in the dark, an immense searching, an immense onslaught, wherein there can be no advance save at the cost of many setbacks and many wounds. Those who suffer, whatever form their suffering may take, are a living statement of this austere but noble condition: they are simply paying for the advance and the victory of all. They are the men who have fallen on the battlefield.

43

Then it is really true, Lord? By helping on the spread of science and freedom I can increase the density of the divine atmosphere, in itself as well as for me, that atmosphere in which it is always my one desire to be immersed. By laying hold on the earth I enable myself to cling closely to you.

May the kingdom of matter, then, under our scrutinies and our manipulations, surrender to us the secrets of its texture, its movements, its history.

May the world's energies, mastered by us, bow down before us and accept the yoke of our power.

May the race of men, grown to fuller consciousness and greater strength, become grouped into rich and happy organisms in which life shall be put to better use and bring in a hundredfold return.

May the universe offer to our gaze the symbols and the forms of all harmony and all beauty.

I must *search:* and I must *find.*

What is at stake, Lord, is the element wherein you will to dwell here on earth.

What is at stake is your existence amongst us.

44

Let us just consider whether we might not be able to escape from the anxiety into which the dangerous power of thought is now plunging us—simply by improving our thinking still more. And to do this let us begin by climbing up till we tower over the trees which now hide the forest from us; in other words let us forget for a moment the details of the economic crises, the political tensions, the class struggles which block out our horizon, and let us climb high enough to gain an inclusive and impartial view of the whole process of *hominization**

---

* *Hominization* is Père Teilhard's term for what Sir Julian Huxley has called "progressive psychosocial evolution," i.e., the process whereby mankind's potentialities are more and more fully realized in the world, and all the forces contained in the animal world are progressively spiritualized in human civilization. (Tr. note.)

as it has advanced during the last fifty or sixty years.

From this vantage point what do we *first* notice? And if some observer were to come to us from one of the stars what would he *chiefly* notice?

Without question, two major phenomena:

the first, that in the course of half a century technology has advanced with incredible rapidity, an advance not just of scattered, localized technical developments but of a real *geotechnology* which spreads out the close-woven network of its interdependent enterprises over the totality of the earth;

the second, that in the same period, at the same pace and on the same scale of planetary cooperation and achievement, *science* has transformed in every direction—from the infinitesimal to the immense and to the immensely complex—our common vision of the world and our common power of action.

45

Lord, what is there in suffering that commits me so deeply to you?

Why should my wings flutter more joyfully than before when you stretch out nets to imprison me?

It is because, among your gifts, what I hanker after is the fragrance of your power over me and the touch of your hand upon me. For what exhilarates us human creatures more than freedom, more than the glory of achievement, is the joy of finding and surrendering to a Beauty greater than man, the rapture of being possessed.

Blessed then be the disappointments which snatch the cup from our lips; blessed be the chains which force us to go where we would not.

Blessed be relentless time and the unending thraldom in which it holds us: the inexorable bondage of time that goes too slowly and frets our impatience, of time that goes too quickly and ages us, of time that never stops, and never returns.

Blessed, above all, be death and the horror of falling back through death into the cosmic forces. At the moment of its coming a power as strong as the universe pounces upon our bodies to grind them to dust and dissolve them, and an attraction more tremendous than any material tension draws our unresisting souls towards their proper center. Death causes us to lose our footing completely in ourselves so as to deliver us over to the powers of heaven and earth. This is its final terror—but it is also, for the mystic, the climax of his bliss.

God's creative power does not in fact fashion us as though out of soft clay: it is a fire that kindles life in whatever it touches, a quickening spirit. Therefore it is *during our lifetime* that we must decisively adapt ourselves to it, model ourselves upon it, identify ourselves with it. The mystic is given at times a keen, obsessive insight into this situation. And anyone who has this insight, and who loves, will feel within himself a fever of active dependence and of arduous purity seizing upon him and driving him on to an absolute integrity and the complete utilization of all his powers.

In order to become perfectly resonant to the pulsations of the basic rhythm of reality the mystic makes himself docile to the least hint of human obligation, the most unobtrusive demands of grace.

To win for himself a little more of the creative energy, he tirelessly develops his thought, dilates his heart, intensifies his external activity. For created beings must work if they would be yet further created.

And finally, that no blemish may separate him, by so much as a single atom of himself, from the essential limpidity, he labors unceasingly to purify his affections and to remove even the very faintest opacities which might cloud or impede the light.

46

Where human holiness offers itself as a means to his ends, God is not content to send forth in greater intensity his creative influence, the child of his power: he himself comes down into his work to consolidate its unification. He told us this, he and no other. The more the soul's desires are concentrated on him, the more he will flood into them, penetrate their depths and draw them into his own irresistible simplicity. Between those who love one another with true charity he appears—he is, as it were, *born*—as a substantial bond of their love.

It is God himself who rises up in the heart of this simplified world. And the organic form of the universe thus divinized is Christ Jesus, who, through the magnetism of his love and the effective power of his Eucharist, gradually gathers into himself all the unitive energy scattered through his creation.

Christ consumes with his glance my entire being.

And with that same glance, that same presence, he enters into those who are around me and whom I love. Thanks to him therefore I am united with them, as in a divine *milieu*, through their inmost selves, and I can act upon them with all the resources of my being.

Christ *binds* us and *reveals* us to one another.

What my lips fail to convey to my brother or my sister he will tell them better than I. What my heart desires for them with anxious, helpless ardor he will grant them if it be good. What men cannot hear because of the feebleness of my voice, what they shut their ears against so as not to hear it, this I can confide to Christ who will one day tell it again, to their hearts. And if all this is so I can indeed die with my ideal, I can be buried with the vision I wanted to share with others. Christ gathers up for the life of tomorrow our stifled ambitions, our inadequate understandings, our uncompleted or clumsy but sincere endeavors. *Nunc dimittis, Domine, servum tuum in pace. . . .**

It happens sometimes that a man who is pure of heart will discern in himself, besides the happiness which brings peace to his own individual desires and affections, a quite *special joy, springing from a source outside himself*, which enfolds him in an *immeasurable sense of well-being*. This is the flowing back into his own diminutive personality of the new glow of health which Christ through his incarnation has infused into humanity as a whole: in

---

* "Now thou dost dismiss thy servant, O Lord, in peace." (Luke 2.29.)

him, souls are gladdened with a feeling of warmth, for now they can live in communion with one another. . . .

But if they are to share in this joy and this vision they must first of all have had the courage to break through the narrow confines of their individuality, cease to be egocentric and become Christocentric.

For this is Christ's law, and it is categorical: *Si quis vult post me venire, abneget semetipsum.**

Purity is a basic condition of this self-renouncement and mortification.

And charity much more so.

Once a man has resolved to live generously in love with God and his fellow-men, he realizes that so far he has achieved nothing by the generous renunciations he has made in order to perfect his own inner unity. This unity in its turn must, if it is to be born anew in Christ, suffer an eclipse which will seem to annihilate it. For in truth those will be saved who dare to set the center of their being *outside themselves*, who dare to love Another *more than themselves*, and in some sense become this Other: which is to say, who dare to pass through death to find life. *Si quis vult animam suam salvam facere, perdet eam.***

Clearly, the believer knows that at the price of this sacrifice he is gaining a unity greatly superior to that which he has abandoned. But who can tell

* "If any man will come after me, let him deny himself." (Matt. 16.24.)

** "For whosoever will save his life shall lose it; for he that shall lose his life for my sake, shall save it." (Luke 9.24.)

the anguish of this metamorphosis? Between the moment when he consents to dissolve his inferior unity and that other, rapturous moment when he arrives at the threshold of his new existence, the *real* Christian feels himself to be hovering over an abyss of disintegration and annihilation. The salvation of the soul must be bought at the price of a great risk incurred and accepted: we have, without reservation, to stake earth against heaven; we have to give up the secure and tangible unity of the egocentric life and risk everything on God. "If the grain of wheat does not fall into the ground and die, it remains just a grain."

Therefore when a man is burdened with sorrow, when he falls ill, when he dies, none of those around him can say with certainty whether his being is thereby diminished or increased. For under exactly *the same appearances* the two opposite principles draw to themselves their faithful, leading them either to simplicity or to multiplicity: the two principles which are God and Nothingness.*

47

Egoism, whether personal or racial, has good reason to be thrilled at the idea of an individual element ascending, through its fidelity to life, to the uttermost development of all that is unique and in-

* "The self-conscious death-throes of an eternal decomposition" writes the author elsewhere, of this antipode of God. (Ed. note.)

communicable within itself. Its *instinct* therefore is correct. Its only mistake, but one which causes it to aim in exactly the wrong direction, is to *confuse individuality with personality*. By trying to separate itself as far as possible from others, the element individualizes itself; but in so doing it falls back, and tries to drag the world back into plurality and materiality. In point of fact therefore it dwindles away and is lost. If we are to be fully ourselves we must advance in the opposite direction, towards a convergence with all other beings, towards a union with what is *other* than ourselves. The perfection of our own being, the full achievement of what is unique in each one of us, lies not in our individuality but in our personality; and because of the evolutionary structure of the world we can find that personality only in union with others. There can be no mind without synthesis; and this same law holds good everywhere in created reality, from top to bottom. The true self grows in inverse proportion to the growth of egoism. The element becomes personal only in so far as (in imitation of that Omega point which draws it onwards) it becomes universal.

But there is an obvious and essential proviso to be made. It follows from the foregoing analysis that if the human particles are to become truly personalized under the creative influence of union it is not enough for them to be joined together no matter how. Since what is in question is the achieving of a synthesis of centers it must be center to center and in no other way that they establish contact with one another. Amongst the various forms of psychic interaction which animate the noosphere, therefore, it is the "intercentric" energies that we have above all to identify, to harness and to develop if we would make an effective contribution to the progress of evolution within ourselves.

In other words, the problem to which all this leads us is the problem of love.

48

The sacramental bread is made out of grains of wheat which have been pressed out and ground in the mill; and the dough has been slowly kneaded. Your hands, Lord Jesus, have broken the bread before they hallow it. . . .

Who shall describe, Lord, the violence suffered by the universe from the monent it falls under your sway?

Christ is the goad that urges creatures along the road of effort, of elevation, of development.

He is the sword that mercilessly cuts away such of the body's members as are unworthy or decayed.

He is that mightier life which inexorably brings death to our base egoism so as to draw into itself all our capacities for loving.

That Christ may enter deeply into us we need alternatively the work that dilates the heart and the sorrow that brings death to it, the life that enlarges a man in order that he may be sanctifiable and the death that diminishes him in order that he may be sanctified.

The universe splits in two, it suffers a painful cleavage at the heart of each of its monads, as the flesh of Christ is born and grows. Like the work of creation which it redeems and surpasses, the Incarnation, so desired of man, is an awe-inspiring work: it is achieved through blood.

May the blood of the Lord Jesus—the blood which is infused into creatures and the blood which is shed and spread out over all, the blood of endeavor and the blood of renouncement—mingle with the pain of the world.

*Hic est calix sanguinis mei. . . .**

49

To be pure of heart means to love God above all things and at the same time to see him everywhere in all things. The just man, whether he is rising above and beyond all creatures to an almost immediate awareness of Godhead or throwing himself upon the world—as it is every man's duty to do—to conquer it and bring it to perfection, will have eyes only for God. For him, *objects have lost their surface multiplicity:* in each of them, according to the measure of its own particular qualities and possibilities, God may truly be laid hold on. The pure heart is *of its nature* privileged to move within an immense and superior unity. Who then could fail to see that the effect of this contact with God must be to unify it to the inmost core of its being; and who could fail to divine the inestimable aid that life in its progress will henceforth derive from the Word?

While the sinner, by abandoning himself to his

---

* "This is the chalice of my blood. . . ."

appetites, brings about a dispersal and disintegration of his spirit, the saint, by an inverse process, escapes from the complexities of affection and in so doing he immaterializes himself. For him, God is everything and everything is God, and Christ is at once God and everything. On such an object, which comprises in its simplicity—for the eyes, the heart, the spirit—all the truth and all the beauties of heaven and earth, the soul's faculties converge, touch, are welded together in the flame of a single act which is indistinguishably both vision and love. Thus *the activity proper to purity* (in scholastic terms, its formal effect) is the *unification of the inner powers of the soul* in a single act of appetition of extraordinary richness and intensity. In fine, the pure heart is the heart which, surmounting the multiple and disruptive pull of created things, fortifies its unity (which is to say, matures its spirituality) in the fire of the divine simplicity.

What purity effects in the individual, charity brings about within the community of souls. One cannot but be surprised (when one looks at it with a mind not dulled by habit) at the extraordinary care taken by Christ to urge upon men the importance of loving one another. Mutual love is the Master's new commandment, the distinguishing mark of his disciples, the sure sign of predestination, the principal work to be achieved in all human existence. In the end we shall be judged on love, by love we shall be condemned or justified. . . .

50

We make bold to boast of our age as an age of science. And to a certain extent we are justified, if we are thinking simply in terms of the dawn as opposed to the night which preceded it. Thanks to our discoveries and our methods of research, something of enormous import has been born in the universe, something which I am convinced will now never be stopped. But while we exalt research and profit by it, with what pettiness of mind, what paltry means, what disorderly methods, do we still today pursue our researches!

Have we ever given serious thought to our sorry predicament?

Like art, and one might almost say like thought itself, science seemed at its birth to be but superfluity and fantasy, the product of an exuberant overflow of inward activity beyond the sphere of the material necessities of life, the fruit of the curiosity of dreamers and idlers. Then, little by little, it achieved an importance and an effectiveness which earned for it the freedom of the city. We who live in a world which it can truly be said to have revolutionized acknowledge its social significance and sometimes even make it the object of a cult. Nevertheless we still leave it to grow as best it can, hardly tending it at all, like those wild plants whose fruits are plucked by primitive peoples in their forests.

51

Given a really deep insight into the concept of collectivity, we are bound, I think, to understand the term without any attenuation of meaning, and certainly as no mere metaphor, when we apply it to the sum of all human beings. The immensity of the universe is necessarily homogeneous both in its nature and in its dimensions. Would it still be so if the loops of its spiral were to lose any slightest degree of reality or consistence as they mount higher and higher? The as yet unnamed reality which the gradual combination of individuals, of peoples, of races, will eventually bring into existence in the world must, if it is to be coherent with the rest of reality, be *not infraphysical but supraphysical*. Deeper than the common act of vision in which it expresses itself, and more important than the common power of action from which it emerges by a sort of autogenesis, there is the reality itself to which we must look forward, the reality constituted by the vital union of all the particles endowed with reflective consciousness.

To say this is simply to say (what is indeed probable enough) that the stuff of the universe does not achieve its full evolutionary cycle when it achieves consciousness, and that we are therefore moving on towards some new critical point. In spite of its organic connecting-links, the existence of which is everywhere apparent to us, the biosphere still formed no more than an assemblage of divergent lines, free at their extremities. Then, thanks to reflective thought and the recoils it involves, the lines converge and the loose ends meet: the noosphere becomes a single closed system in which each element individually sees, feels, desires and suffers the same things as all the rest together with them.

Thus we have a harmonized collectivity of consciousnesses which together make up a sort of superconsciousness; the earth not merely covered by myriads of grains of thought but enclosed in one single enveloping consciousness so that it forms, functionally, a single vast grain of thought on a sidereal scale of immensity, the plurality of individual acts of reflective consciousness coming together and reinforcing one another in a single unanimous act.

Such is the general form in which, by analogy and in symmetry with the past, we are led scientifically to envisage that humanity of the future in which alone the terrestrial drives implicit in our activity can find a terrestrial fulfillment.

52

You know, my God, that I can now scarcely discern in the world the lineaments of its multiplicity; for when I gaze at it I see it chiefly as a limitless reservoir in which the two contrary energies of joy and suffering are accumulating in vast quantities—and for the most part lying unused.

And I see how through this restless, wavering mass there pass powerful psychic currents made up of souls who are carried away by a passion for art, for love, for science and the mastery of the universe, for the autonomy of the individual, for the freedom of mankind.

From time to time these currents collide one with another in formidable crises which cause them to seethe and foam in their efforts to establish their equilibrium.

What glory it were for you, my God, and what an affluence of life to your humanity, could all this spiritual power be harmonized in you!

Lord, to see drawn from so much wealth, lying unused or put to base uses, all the dynamism that is locked up within it: this is my dream. And to share in bringing this about: this is the work to which I would dedicate myself .

As far as I can, *because I am a priest,* I would henceforth be the first to become aware of what the world loves, pursues, suffers. I would be the first to seek, to sympathize, to toil; the first in self-fulfillment, the first in self-denial. For the sake of the world I would be more widely human in my sympathies and more nobly terrestrial in my ambitions than any of the world's servants.

On the one hand I want to plunge into the midst of created things and, mingling with them, seize hold upon and disengage from them all that they contain of life eternal, down to the very last fragment, so that nothing may be lost; and on the other hand I want, by practicing the counsels of perfection, to salvage through their self-denials all the heavenly fire imprisoned within the three-fold concupiscence of the flesh, of avarice, of pride: in other words to hallow, through chastity, poverty and obedience, the power enclosed in love, in gold, in independence.

That is why I have clothed my vows and my priesthood (and it is this that gives me my strength and my happiness) in a determination to accept and to divinize the powers of the earth.

53

Show all your faithful followers, Lord, in how real and complete a sense *opera sequuntur illos,* their works follow after them into your kingdom. Otherwise they will be like indolent workmen who find no spur to action in a task to be achieved; or else, if a healthy human instinct overrides their hesitancies or the fallacies they derive from a misunderstanding of religion, they will still be a prey to a fundamental division and frustration within themselves, and it will be said that the sons of heaven cannot, on the human level, compete with true conviction and therefore on equal terms with the children of this world.

54

In the Christian vision, the great triumph of the Creator and Redeemer is to have transformed into an essential agent of life bestowal what in itself is a universal power of diminishment and extinction. If God is definitively to enter into us, he must in some way hollow us out, empty us, so as to make room for himself. And if we are to be assimilated into him, he must first break down the molecules of our being so as to recast and remold us. It is the function of death to make the necessary opening into our inmost selves. Death brings about in us the required dissociation; death puts us into that state which is organically necessary if the divine fire is to descend upon us. And thus its baneful power to bring about decomposition and dissolution is harnessed to the most sublime of life's activities. What was of its nature void, empty, a regression into plurality, can now in every human being become plenitude and unity in God.

55

The divinizing of our efforts through the value of the intention we put into them infuses into all our actions a *soul* of great price, but *it does not confer on their bodies the hope of resurrection.* Yet that hope is a necessity if our joy is to be complete. True, it is no small thing to be able to reflect that, if we love God, something of our inner activity, our *operatio*, will never perish. But what of the results of that activity, the products of our minds and hearts and hands, our achievements, our *opus:* shall not these too be in some way preserved, "eternalized"?

Indeed, Lord, yes, it will be so, in virtue of a claim which you yourself have implanted in the depths of my will. I want it to be so, I need that it should be so.

I want it because I cannot help loving all that your constant help enables me each day to bring into being. A thought, a harmony, the achievement of a perfection in material things, some special *nuance* in human love, the exquisite complexity of a smile or a glance, every new embodiment of beauty appearing in me or around me on the human face of the earth: I cherish them all like children whose flesh I cannot believe destined to complete extinction. If I believed that these things were to perish for ever, would I have given them life? The deeper I look into myself the more clearly I become aware of this psychological truth: that no man would lift his little finger to attempt the smallest task unless he were spurred on by a more or less obscure conviction that in some infinitesimally tiny way he is contributing, at least indirectly, to the building up of something permanent—in other words, to your own work, Lord.

56

But, once again, we must tell ourselves: "In truth I say to you: only the daring can enter the kingdom of God, hidden henceforth in the heart of the world."

It is of no use to read these pages, or other similar pages written twenty centuries ago, merely with one's eyes. Anyone who, without having put his hand to the plough, thinks he has mastered them is deluding himself. *We must try to live them.*

If we would form an idea of the active power of faith and of what it achieves we must have struggled long and patiently: we must, in view of the practical uncertainty of the morrow, have thrown ourselves, in a true act of inward submission, upon

Providence considered as being as physically real as the objects of our disquietude; we must, in our suffering of the ills we have incurred, our remorse for sins we have committed, our vexation over the opportunities we have missed, have forced ourselves to believe unhesitatingly that God is powerful enough to turn each and every particular evil into good; we must, despite appearances to the contrary, have acted without reservation as though chastity, humility, gentleness were the only directions in which our being could make progress; we must, in the penumbra of death, have forced ourselves not to look back to the past but to seek in utter darkness the love of God.

Only he who has fought bravely and been victorious in the struggle against the spurious security and strength and attraction of the past can attain to the firm and blissful *experiential certainty* that the more we lose all foothold in the darkness and instability of the future, the more deeply we penetrate into God.

57

No, Lord, you do not ask of me anything that is false or beyond my power to achieve. Through your self-revealing and the power of your grace you simply compel what is most human in us to become at long last aware of itself. Humanity has been sleeping—and still sleeps—lulled within the narrowly confining joys of its little closed loves. In the depths of the human multitude there slumbers an immense spiritual power which will manifest itself only when we have learned how to *break through the dividing walls* of our egoism and raise ourselves up to an entirely new perspective, so that habitually and in a practical fashion we fix our gaze on the universal realities.

Lord Jesus, you who are the Savior of our human activity because you bring us a motive for acting, and the Savior of our human pain because you endow it with a life-giving value: be also the Savior of our human unity by compelling us to repudiate all our pettiness and, relying on you, to venture forth on to the uncharted ocean of charity.

IN THE TOTAL CHRIST

58

Since Jesus was born, and grew to his full stature, and died, everything has continued to move forward *because Christ is not yet fully formed:* he has not yet gathered about him the last folds of his robe of flesh and of love which is made up of his faithful followers. The mystical Christ has not yet attained to his full growth; and therefore the same is true of the cosmic Christ. Both of these are simultaneously in the state of being and of becoming; and it is from the prolongation of this process of becoming that all created activity ultimately springs. Christ is the end point of the evolution, even the *natural* evolution, of all beings; and therefore evolution is holy.

59

In manus tuas commendo spiritum meum. * Into
the hands which broke and quickened the bread,
which blessed and caressed little children, which
were pierced with the nails; into the hands which
are like our hands, the hands of which one can
never tell what they will do with the object they
are holding, whether they will break it or heal it,
but which we know will always obey and reveal
impulses filled with kindness and will always clasp
us ever more closely, ever more jealously; into the
gentle and mighty hands which can reach down
into the very depth of the soul, the hands which
fashion, which create, the hands through which
flows out so great a love: into these hands it is com-
forting to surrender oneself, especially if one is
suffering or afraid. And there is both great happiness and great merit in so doing.

60

It is the whole of my being, Lord Jesus, that you
would have me give you, tree and fruit alike, the
finished work as well as the harnessed power, the
opus together with the *operation*. To allay your
hunger and slake your thirst, to nourish your body
and bring it to its full stature, you need to find in
us a substance which will truly be food for you.
And this food ready to be transformed into you,
this nourishment for your flesh, I will prepare for

---

* "Into thy hands I commend my spirit." (Luke 23.46.)

you by liberating the spirit in myself and in every-thing:

through an effort (even a purely natural effort) to learn the truth, to live the good, to create the beautiful;

through cutting away all inferior and evil energies;

through practicing that charity towards all men which alone can gather up the multitude into a single soul. . . .

To promote, in however small a degree, *the awakening of spirit in the world* is to offer to the incarnate Word an *increase of reality and stability;* it is to allow his influence to grow in intensity around us.

61

Through everything in me that has subsistence and resonance, everything that enlarges me from within, everything that arouses me, attracts me, wounds me from without: through all these, Lord, you work upon me, you mold and spiritualize my formless clay, you transform me into yourself.

In order to take possession of me, my God, you who are so much more remote in your immensity and so much deeper in the intimacy of your indwelling than all things else, you take to yourself and unite together the immensity of the world and the intimate depths of my being: and I am conscious of bearing deep within me all the strain and struggle of the universe.

But, Lord, I do not just passively give way to

these blessed passivities: I offer myself to them, actively, and do all I can to promote them.

I know how the life-giving power of the host can be blocked by our freedom of will. If I seal up the entry into my heart I must dwell in darkness—and not only I, my individual soul, but the whole universe in so far as its activity sustains my organism and awakens my consciousness, and in so far also as I act upon it in my turn so as to draw forth from it the materials of sensation, of ideas, of moral goodness, of holiness of life. But if on the other hand my heart is open to you, then at once through the pure intent of my will the divine must flood into the universe in so far as the universe is centered on me. Since, by virtue of my consent, I shall have become a living particle of the body of Christ, all that affects me must in the end help on the growth of the total Christ. Christ will flood into me and over me, me and *my* cosmos.

How I long, Lord Christ, for this to be!

May my acceptance be ever more complete, more comprehensive, more intense!

May my being, in its self-offering to you, become ever more open and more transparent to your influence!

And may I thus feel your activity coming ever closer, your presence growing ever more intense, everywhere around me.

Fiat, fiat.

62

If we look at the world simultaneously from an evolutionary and a spiritual point of view we shall see it as being a tremendous responsibility but also, even at the lowliest stages of belief in God, we shall see it as glowing with an irresistible attraction. For then it is not just a few privileged creatures that are seen as capable of satisfying each man's essential need of finding something to love him and complement him: it is, thanks to these few and as a sort of reflection of them, the sum total of all the beings engaged together with him in the unifying work of the cosmos. In the last resort each element can find its beatitude only in union with the totality and with the transcendent Center required to set the totality in motion. Consequently, if it is not possible for him, psychologically to surround each being with that particular, overflowing affection which characterizes our human love, at least he can nurture in his heart that generalized but none the less real affection for all that is which will cause him to cherish in each thing, over and above its surface qualities, the being itself—that is to say, that indefinable, elect part of each thing which, under God's influence, gradually becomes flesh of his flesh.

Such a love has no exact equivalent among the various kinds of attachment to be found in our ordinary human relationships. Its "material object" (as the Schoolmen would say)* is so immense and

* The material object of (for instance) a science is the subject matter, in general, with which it is concerned; its for-

its "formal object" so profound that it can be expressed only in terms at once of marriage and of adoration. In it, all distinction between egoism and disinterestedness tends to evaporate. Each one loves himself and seeks his own fulfillment in the fulfillment of all the rest; and the least gesture of possession turns into an effort to attain, in the far-distant future, to what shall be the same in all.

63

Henceforth we know enough—and it is already a great deal—to be able to say that these onward gropings of life will succeed only in one condition: that the whole endeavor shall have unity as its keynote. Of its very nature the advance of the biological process demands this. Outside this atmosphere of a union glimpsed and longed for, the most legitimate demands are bound to lead to catastrophe: we can see this only too clearly at the present moment. On the other hand, once this atmosphere is created almost any solution will seem as good as all the others, and every sort of effort will succeed, at least in the beginning. Thus, if in dealing with the problem of the various human races, their appearance, their awakening, their future, we start from its purely biological roots, it will lead us to recognize that the only climate in which man can con-

---

mal object is the specific aspect under which that subject matter is studied. Thus man is the material object alike of anthropology, psychology, physiology and so on, the formal object being different in each case.

tinue to grow is that of devotion and self-denial in a spirit of brotherhood. In truth, at the rate the consciousness and the ambitions of the world are increasing, it will explode unless it learns to love. The future of the thinking earth is organically bound up with the turning of the forces of hate into forces of charity.

64

Though the phenomena of the lower world remain the same—the material determinisms, the vicissitudes of chance, the laws of labor, the agitations of men, the footfalls of death—he who *dares* to believe reaches a sphere of created reality in which things, while retaining their habitual texture, seem to be made out of a different substance. Everything remains the same so far as phenomena are concerned, but at the same time everything becomes luminous, animated, loving. . . .

Through the workings of faith, Christ appears, Christ is born, without any violation of nature's laws, in the heart of the world.

65

As the years go by, Lord, I come to see more and more clearly, in myself and in those around me, that the great secret preoccupation of modern man is much less to battle for possession of the world than to find a means of escaping from it. The anguish of feeling that one is not merely spatially but ontologically imprisoned in the cosmic bubble; the anxious search for an issue to, or more exactly a focal point for, the evolutionary process: these are the prices we must pay for the growth of planetary consciousness; these are the dimly-recognized burdens which weigh down the souls of Christian and gentile alike in the world of today.

Now that humanity has become conscious of the movement which carries it onwards it has more and more need of finding, above and beyond itself, an infinite objective, an infinite issue, to which it can wholly dedicate itself.

And what is this infinity? The effect of twenty centuries of mystical travail has been precisely to show us that the Baby of Bethlehem, the Man on the Cross, is also the Principle of all movement and the unifying Center of the world: how then can we fail to identify this God not merely of the old cosmos but also of the new cosmogenesis, this God so greatly sought after by our generation, with you, Lord Jesus, you who make him visible to our eyes and bring him close to us?

66

Let us leave the surface and, without leaving the world, plunge into God. There, and from there, in him and through him we shall hold all things and have command of all things, we shall find again the essence and the splendor of all the flowers, the lights, we have had to surrender here and now in order to be faithful to life. Those beings whom here and now we despair of ever reaching and influencing, they too will be there, united together at that central point in their being which is at once the most vulnerable, the most receptive and the most enriching. There, even the least of our desires and our endeavors will be gathered and preserved, and be able to evoke instantaneous vibration from the very heart of the universe.

Let us then establish ourselves in the divine *milieu*. There, we shall be within the inmost depths of souls and the greatest consistency of matter. There, at the confluence of all the forms of beauty, we shall discover the ultravital, ultraperceptible, ultraactive point of the universe; and, at the same time, we shall experience in the depths of our own being the effortless deployment of the *plenitude* of all our powers of action and of adoration.

For it is not merely that at that privileged point all the external springs of the world are coordinated and harmonized: there is the further, complementary marvel that the man who surrenders himself to the divine *milieu* feels his own inward powers directed and enlarged by it with a sureness which enables him effortlessly to avoid the all too numerous reefs on which mystical quests have so often foundered.

67

Lord, once again I ask: which is the more precious of these two beatitudes, that all things are means through which I can touch you, or that you yourself are so "universal" that I can experience you and lay hold on you in every creature?

Some think to make you more lovable in my eyes

by praising almost exclusively the charm and the
kindness of your human face as men saw it long
ago on earth. But if I sought only a human being to
cherish, would I not turn to those whom you have
given me here and now in all the charm of their
flowering? Do we not all have around us irresistibly
lovable mothers, brothers, sisters, friends? Why
should we go searching the Judaea of two thousand
years ago? No, what I cry out for, like every other
creature, with my whole being, and even with all
my passionate earthly longings, is something very
different from an equal to cherish: It is a God to
adore.

68

Lord Jesus, Master before whose beauty and all-
demanding love we have cause to tremble: turning
my eyes away from what my human weakness cannot as yet understand and therefore cannot bear to
think about—the idea that there are in reality souls
eternally damned*—I would at least make the constant somber menace of damnation a part of my habitual and practical vision of the world, not so
much in order to fear you, but rather in order to
become more passionately surrendered to you.

* According to Catholic teaching, the existence of hell, of a
state of eternal damnation, is an article of faith (as indeed,
given free will and evil, it is a logical necessity); but that
some human beings are or will be in fact damned is not an
article of faith (though again logically it must be regarded
as a possibility): hence Père Teilhard's prayer further on in
this passage. (Tr. note.)

A moment ago I cried out to you: be to me, Lord Jesus, not only a brother, but a God. And now, panoplied as you are in that fearsome power of choosing and rejecting which places you at the world's summit as principle of universal attraction and universal repulsion, now you do truly appear to me as that vast and vital force which I sought everywhere that I might adore it. And now I realize that the fires of hell and the fires of heaven are not two different forces but are contrary manifestations of one and the same energy.

Let not the hell-flames touch me, Master, nor any of those I love, nor indeed anyone at all (and I know, my Lord and God, that you will forgive me the audacity of my prayer), but may their somber glow, and all the abysses they reveal, be for each and all of us incorporated into the blazing plenitude of your divine *milieu.*

69

Lift up your head, Jerusalem, and see the immense multitude of those who build and those who seek; see all those who toil in laboratories, in studios, in factories, in the deserts and in the vast crucible of human society. For all the ferment produced by their labors, in art, in science, in thought, all is for you.

Therefore open wide your arms, open wide your heart, and like Christ your Lord welcome the wave-flow, the flood, of the sap of humanity. Take it to yourself, for without its baptism you will wither away for lack of longing as a flower withers for lack of water; and preserve it and care for it, since without your sun it will go stupidly to waste in sterile shoots.

What has become of the temptations aroused by a world too vast in its horizons, too seductive in its beauty?

They no longer exist.

The earth mother can indeed take me now into the immensity of her arms. She can enlarge me with her life, or take me back into her primordial dust. She can adorn herself for me with every allurement, every horror, every mystery. She can intoxicate me with the scent of her tangibility and her unity. She can throw me to my knees in expectancy of what is maturing in her womb.

But all her enchantments can no longer harm me, since she has become for me, more than herself and beyond herself, the body of him who is and who is to come.

70

To read the gospel with an open mind is to see beyond all possibility of doubt that Jesus came to bring us new truths concerning our destiny: not only a new life superior to that we are conscious of, but also in a very real sense a new physical power of acting upon our *temporal* world.

Through a failure to grasp the exact nature of this power newly bestowed on all who put their confidence in God—a failure due either to a hesitation in face of what seems to us so unlikely or to a fear of falling into illuminism—many Christians neglect this earthly aspect of the promises of the Master, or at least do not give themselves to it with that complete hardihood which he nevertheless never tires of asking of us, if only we have ears to hear him.

We must not allow timidity or modesty to turn us into poor craftsmen. If it is true that the development of the world can be influenced by our faith in Christ, then to let this power lie dormant within us would indeed be unpardonable.

71

God, who cannot in any way blend or be mingled with the creation which he sustains and animates and binds together, is nonetheless present in the birth, the growth and the consummation of all things.

The earthly undertaking which is beyond all parallel is the physical incorporation of the faithful into Christ and therefore into God. And this supreme work is carried out with the *exactitude and the harmony of a natural process of evolution.*

At the inception of the undertaking there had to be a transcendent act which, in accordance with mysterious but physically regulated conditions, should graft the person of a God into the human cosmos. This was the Incarnation: *Et Verbum caro factum est.** And from this first, basic contact of God with our human race, and precisely by virtue of this penetration of the divine into our human na-

---

* "And the Word was made Flesh." (John 1.14.)

ture, a new life was born: that unforeseeable aggrandizement and "obediential"* extension of our natural capacities which we call "grace." Now grace is the sap which, rising in the one trunk, spreads through all the veins in obedience to the pulsations of the one heart; it is the nerve-impulse flowing through all the members at the command of the one brain; and the radiant Head, the mighty Heart, the fruitful Tree are, of necessity, Christ.

The Incarnation means the renewal, the restoration, of all the energies and powers of the universe; Christ is the instrument, the Center and the End of all creation, animate *and* material; through him everything is created, hallowed, quickened. This is the constant, *general* teaching of St John and St Paul (that most "cosmic" of sacred writers), a teaching which has passed into the most solemn phrases of the liturgy, but which we repeat and which future generations will go on repeating to the end without ever being able to master or to measure its profound and mysterious meaning, bound up as it is with the comprehension of the universe.

72

Only love can bring individual beings to their perfect completion, as individuals, by uniting them

---

* An obediential potentiality is one whose actualization goes beyond the natural, innate limitations of its subject, while not being irreconcilable with those limitations, e.g. the direct intuition of God in the beatific vision. (Tr. note.)

one with another, because only loves takes possession of them and unites them by what lies deepest within them. This is simply a fact of our everyday experience. For indeed at what moment do lovers come into the most complete possession of themselves if not when they say they are lost in one another? And is not love all the time achieving—in couples, in teams, all around us—the magical and reputedly contradictory feat of personalizing through totalizing? And why should not what is thus daily achieved on a small scale be repeated one day on worldwide dimensions?

Humanity, the spirit of the earth, the synthesis of individuals and peoples, the paradoxical conciliation of the element with the whole, of the one with the many: all these are regarded as utopian fantasies, yet they are biologically necessary; and if we would see them made flesh in the world what more need we do than imagine our power to love growing and broadening till it can embrace the totality of men of the earth?

73

You, Lord Jesus, are the epitome and the crown of all perfection, human and cosmic. No flash of beauty, no enchantment of goodness, no element of force, but finds in you the ultimate refinement and consummation of itself. To possess you is in truth to hold gathered into a single object the perfect assemblage of all that the universe can give us and make us dream of. The unique savor of the glory and wonder of your being has so effectively drawn out from the earth and synthetized all the most exquisite savors that the earth contains or can suggest that now we can find them, endlessly, one after another according to our desires, in you—you the Bread that "holds within it every delight."

You who are yourself the *plenitudo entis creati,* the fullness of created being, Lord Jesus, are also the *plenitudo entis mei,* the fullness of my own personal being, and of all living creatures who accept your dominion. In you and in you alone, as in a boundless abyss, our powers can launch forth into activity and find surcease for their tensions, can show their full capacity without encountering any limitation, can plunge into love and into the wild abandon of love with the certainty of finding in your depths no wreck-rocks of failure, no shallows of pettiness, no currents of perverted truth.

By you and by you alone, who are the entire and proper object of our love and the creative energy that fathoms the secrets of our hearts and the mystery of our growth, our souls are awakened, sensitized, enlarged, to the utmost limit of their latent potentialities.

And under your influence and yours alone, the sheath of organic isolation and of willful egoism which separates the monads from one another is cleft asunder and dissolves, and the multitude of souls rush on towards that union which is necessary for the maturity of the world.

Thus a third plenitude is added to the other two. In a very real sense, Lord Jesus, you are the *plenitudo entium,* the full assemblage of all the beings who shelter, and meet and are forever united, within the mystical bonds of your body. In your breast, my God, better than in any embrace, I possess all those whom I love and who are illumined by your beauty and in their turn illumine you with the rays of light (so powerful in their effect on our hearts) which they receive from you and send back to you. That multitude of beings, so daunting in its magnitude, that I so long to help, to enlighten, to lead to you: it is already there, Lord, gathered together within you. Through you I can reach into the inmost depths of every being and endow them with whatever I will—provided that I know how to ask you, and that you permit it.

74

The principle of unity which saves our guilty world, wherein all is in process of returning to dust, is Christ. Through the force of his magnetism, the light of his ethical teaching, the unitive power of his very being, Jesus establishes again at the heart of the world the harmony of all endeavors and the convergence of all beings. Let us read the gospel boldly and we shall see that no idea can better convey to our minds the *redemptive function of the Word* than that of a unification of all flesh in one and the same Spirit.

Jesus clothed his divine personality alike in the most palpable and in the most inward beauty and charm of human individuality. He adorned this humanity with the most enchanting and captivating splendors of the universe. And then he came amongst us and showed himself to us as that which we could never have thought to see: the synthesis of all perfections so that now each man must of necessity see him and feel his presence, and must either hate or love what he sees. . . .

75

Lord God, when I go up to your altar for communion, grant that I may derive from it a discernment of the infinite perspectives hidden beneath the smallness and closeness of the host in which you are concealed. Already I have accustomed myself to recognize beneath the inertness of the morsel of bread a consuming power which, as the greatest Doctors of your Church have said, far from being absorbed into me, absorbs me into itself. Help me now to overcome that remaining illusion which would make me think of you as touching me only in a limited and momentary way.

I begin to understand: under the sacramental species you touch me first of all through the "accidents" of matter, of the material bread; but then, in consequence of this, you touch me also through the entire universe inasmuch as the entire universe, thanks to that primary influence, ebbs and flows over me. In a true sense the arms and the heart which you open to me are nothing less than all the united powers of the world which, permeated through and through by your will, your inclinations, your temperament, bend over my being to form it and feed it and draw it into the blazing center of your infinite fire. In the host, Lord Jesus, you offer me *my life*.

76

We who are Christ's disciples must not hesitate to harness this force—the world's expectancy and ferment and unfolding—which needs us and which we need. On the contrary, under pain of allowing it to be dissipated and of perishing ourselves, we must share in those aspirations, in essence authentically religious, which make men today so intensely aware of the immensity of the world, the grandeur of the mind and the sacred value of every newly discovered truth. This is the schooling which will teach our present Christian generation how to await the future.

We have long been profoundly aware of these perspectives: the progress of the universe, and especially the human universe, does not take place in rivalry with God, nor is it a vain squandering of the energies we owe to him. The greater man becomes and the more humanity becomes one, conscious of its power and able to control it, the more beautiful creation will be, the more perfect adoration will become, and the more Christ will find, for the mystical extensions of his humanity, a body worthy of resurrection. The world can no more have two summits of fulfillment than a circumference can have two centers. The star which the world is awaiting though it does not as yet know its name, though it cannot as yet appreciate exactly its transcendence, cannot even distinguish the most spiritual, the most divine of its rays: this star cannot be other than that very Christ in whom we hope. To look with longing to the Parousia of the

Son of Man we have only to allow to beat within our breasts—and to Christianize—the heart of the world.

77

Death will not simply throw us back into the great flux of reality, as the pantheist's picture of beatitude would have us believe. Nevertheless in death we are caught up, overwhelmed, dominated by that divine power which lies within the forces of inner disintegration and, above all, within that irresistible yearning which will drive the separated soul on to complete its further, predestined journey as infallibly as the sun causes the mists to rise from the water on which it shines. Death surrenders us completely to God; it makes us pass into God. In return we have to surrender ourselves to it, in love and in the abandon of love, since, when death comes to us, there is nothing further for us to do but let ourselves be entirely dominated and led onwards by God.

78

Because, Lord, by every innate impulse and through all the hazards of my life I have been driven ceaselessly to search for you and to set you in the heart of the universe of matter, I shall have the joy, when death comes, of closing my eyes amidst the splendor of a universal transparency aglow with fire. . . .

It is as if the fact of bringing together and connecting the two poles, tangible and intangible, external and internal, of the world which bears us onwards had caused everything to burst into flames and set everything free.

In the guise of a tiny baby in its mother's arms, obeying the great laws of birth and infancy, you came, Lord Jesus, to dwell in my infant-soul; and then, as you reenacted in me—and in so doing extended the range of—your growth through the Church, that same humanity which once was born and dwelt in Palestine began now to spread out gradually everywhere like an iridescence of unnumbered hues through which, without destroying anything, your presence penetrated—and endued with supervitality—every other presence about me.

And all this took place because, in a universe which was disclosing itself to me as structurally convergent, you, by right of your resurrection, had assumed the dominating position of all-inclusive Center in which everything is gathered together.

79

Your call, my God, as it comes to men has innumerable different shades of meaning: each vocation is essentially different from all the rest.

The various regions, nations, social groupings, have each their particular apostles.

And I, Lord God, for my (very lowly) part, would wish to be the apostle—and, if I dare say so, the evangelist—of your *Christ in the universe*.

For you gave me the gift of sensing, beneath the incoherence of the surface, the deep, living unity which your grace has mercifully thrown over our heart breaking plurality.

The universality of your divine magnetism, and the intrinsic value of our human undertakings: this, my God, is the twofold truth you have shown me, and I am burning to spread abroad the knowledge of it and to bring it fully into effect.

If you judge me worthy, Lord God, I would show to those whose lives are dull and drab the limitless horizons opening out to humble and hidden efforts; for these efforts, if pure in intention, can add to the extension of the incarnate Word a further element—an element known to Christ's heart and gathered up into his immortality.

You disclosed to me the essential vocation of the world: to attain to its completion, through a chosen part of its whole being, in the plenitude of the incarnate Word.

In order to take possession of me, my God, you who are so much more remote in your immensity and so much deeper in the intimacy of your indwelling than all things else, you take to yourself and unite together the immensity of the world and the intimate depths of my being.

I realize that the totality of all perfections, even natural perfections, is then necessary basis for that mystical and ultimate organism which you are constructing out of all things. You do not destroy, Lord, the beings you adopt for your building; but you transform them while preserving everything good that the centuries of creation have fashioned in them.

The whole world is concentrated and uplifted in expectancy of union with the divine; yet at the same time it encounters an insurmountable barrier. For nothing can come to Christ unless he himself takes it and gathers it into himself.

Toward Christ all the immortal monads converge. Not a single atom, however lowly or imperfect, but must cooperate—at least by way of repulsion or reflection—in the fulfillings of Christ.

Only sin is excluded from the Pleroma. And even so, since to be damned is not to be annihilated, who shall say what mysterious complement might be given to the body of Christ by that immortal loss?

Through their diminution *in Christo Jesu,* those who mortify themselves, who suffer, who bear old age with patience, cross over the critical threshold where death is turned into life. Through forgetting the self they are given to find it, never to lose it again.

The universe takes on the lineaments of Jesus; but then there is great mystery: for he who thus becomes discernible is Jesus crucified.

Christ is loved as a person; he compels recognition as a world.

80

Lord Jesus, when it was given me to see where the dazzling trail on particular beauties and partial harmonies was leading, I recognized that it was all coming to center on a single point, a single person: yourself. Every presence makes me feel that you are near me; every touch is the touch of your hand; every necessity transmits to me a pulsation of your will.

That the Spirit may always shine forth in me, that I may not succumb to the temptation that lies in wait for every act of boldness, nor ever forget that *you alone* must be sought in and through everything, you, Lord, will send me—at what moments only you know—deprivations, disappointments, sorrow.

What is to be brought about is more than a simple union: it is a *transformation,* in the course of which the only thing our human activity can do is, humbly, to make ourselves ready, and to accept.

Seeing the mystic immobile, crucified or rapt in prayer, some may perhaps think that his activity is in abeyance or has left this earth: they are mistaken. Nothing in the world is more intensely alive and active than purity and prayer, which hang like an unmoving light between the universe and God. Through their serene transparency flow the waves of creative power, charged with natural virtue and with grace. What else but this is the Virgin Mary?

81

Christian love, Christian charity: I know from experience how for the most part these words evoke in non-Christians either a kindly or a malicious incredulity. The idea of loving God and the world, they object, is surely a psychological absurdity. How is one in fact to love the intangible, the universal? And then in so far as it can be said more or less metaphorically that a love of all and of the All is possible, is not this inward activity, far from being specifically Christian, familiar to the mystics of India or Persia and to many more?

And yet, are not the facts there before our eyes, physically, almost brutally, to prove the contrary?

In the first place, say what one will, a love, a *true* love of God is perfectly possible: were it not, all the monasteries and all the churches on earth would be emptied in a moment, and Christianity, for all its framework of ritual, of precepts, of hierarchy, would quite inevitably crumble away into nothingness.

In the second place, this love certainly has in Christianity a strength which is not found elsewhere: otherwise, despite all the virtues and all the attraction of the tenderness which characterizes the gospel, the doctrine of the beatitudes and of the Cross would long since have given place to some other, more winning, creed—and more particularly to some form of humanism or belief in purely earthly values.

Whatever the merits of other religions, it remains an undeniable fact—explain it how one will—that the most ardent and most massive blaze of collective love that has ever appeared in the world burns here and now in the heart of the Church of God.

SOURCES OF THE PENSÉES

The Presence of God in the World

1. *La Vie Cosmique*, March 24, 1916 (unpublished).
2. *Mon Univers*, March 25, 1924 (unpublished). 3.
L'Apparition de l'Homme. 4. *Le Milieu Mystique*,
1917 (unpublished). 5. *Le Milieu Mystique*, 1917
(unpublished). 6. *La Vision du Passé*. 7. *La Vision
du Passé*. 8. *The Phenomenon of Man*. 9. *Le Milieu
Divin*. 10. *Le Milieu Divin*. 11. *Le Milieu Mystique*,
1917 (unpublished). 12. *The Future of Man*. 13.
The Phenomenon of Man. 14. *Le Milieu Divin*. 15.
Le Milieu Divin. 16. *The Future of Man*. 17. *Le
Milieu Divin*. 18. *Le Milieu Mystique*, 1917 (unpublished). 19. *Le Milieu Divin*.

Humanity in Progress

20. *La Signification et la Valeur constructrices de la
Souffrance*, "L'Union Catholique des Malades," 1933.
21. *La Signification et la Valeur constructrices de la
Souffrance*, "L'Union Catholique des Malades," 1933.
22. *La Milieu Mystique*, 1917 (unpublished). 23. *La
Foi qui Opère*, 1918 (unpublished). 24. *The Future
of Man*. 25. *Le Milieu Mystique*, 1917 (unpub-

lished). 26. *Notes de Retraites*, 1944–55 (unpublished). 27. *La Vision du Passé*. 28. *The Phenomenon of Man*. 29. *The Phenomenon of Man*. 30. *Le Milieu Divin*. 31. *The Future of Man*. 32. *La Vision du Passé*. 33. *La Vision du Passé*. 34. *The Phenomenon of Man*. 35. *The Future of Man*. 36. *Le Mystique*, 1917 (unpublished). 37. *Le Milieu Divin*. 38. *Le Milieu Divin*. 39. *Le Milieu Divin*.

The Meaning of Human Endeavor

40. Letter to M.T.-C., of November 13, 1916. 41. *Le Prêtre*, 1918 (unpublished). 42. *La Signification et la Valeur constructrices de la Souffrance*, "L'Union Catholique des Malades," 1933. 43. *Le Milieu Mystique*, 1917 (unpublished). 44. *L'Apparition de L'Homme*. 45. *Le Milieu Mystique*, 1917 (unpublished). 46. *La Lutte contre la Multitude*, 1917 (unpublished). 47. *The Phenomenon of Man*. 48. *Le Prêtre*, 1918 (unpublished). 49. *La Lutte contre La Multitude*, 1917 (unpublished). 50. *The Phenomenon of Man*. 51. *The Phenomenon of Man*. 52. *Le Prêtre*, 1918 (unpublished). 53. *Le Milieu Divin*. 54. *Le Milieu Divin*. 55. *Le Milieu Divin*. 56. *La Foi qui Opère*, 1918 (unpublished). 57. *Le Milieu Divin*.

In the Total Christ

58. *La Vie Cosmique*, March 24, 1916 (unpublished). 59. Letter to M.T.-C., November 23, 1916 (unpublished). 60. *Le Prêtre*, 1918 (unpublished). 61. *Le Prêtre*, 1918 (unpublished). 62. *La Vision du*

Passé. 63. *La Vision du Passé.* 64. *La Foi qui Opère,* 1918 (unpublished). 65. *Le Coeur de la Matière,* 1950 (unpublished). 66. *Le Milieu Divin.* 67. *Le Milieu Divin.* 68. *Le Milieu Divin.* 69. *Le Milieu Divin.* 70. *La Foi qui Opère,* 1918 (unpublished). 71. *La Vie Cosmique,* March 24, 1916 and *The Future of Man.* 72. *The Phenomenon of Man.* 73. *Le Prêtre,* 1918 (unpublished). 74. *La Lutte contre la Multitude,* 1917 (unpublished). 75. *Le Milieu Divin.* 76. *Le Milieu Divin.* 77. Letter to M.T.-C., November 13, 1916. 78. *Le Coeur de la Matière,* 1950 (unpublished). 79. *Le Prêtre,* 1918 (unpublished), *passim.* 80. *Le Milieu Mystique,* 1917 (unpublished), *passim.* 81. *Le Christique,* 1955 (unpublished).